FEMININE SPIRITS & ANGELS

Dr. Harry Assad Salem III

FEMININE SPIRITS & ANGELS
ISBN 1-890370-41-X

Salem Family Ministries
PO Box 1595
Cathedral City, CA 92234
www.salemfamilyministries.org

Disclaimer: The views expressed in this book contain personal opinions, theories, experiences, and facts from time spent in God's Word and private research. The versions and translations of the Bibles used throughout the book at times spells the ending of the word Psalms either with *s* or without depending on the various versions and translations of the Bible and is not a personal expression of end of word spelling by the author. Any references to political or social movements are strictly for research and observation purposes.

CONTENTS

"SHE CONQUERED HER DEMONS AND
WORE HER SCARS LIKE WINGS."
-ATTICUS

FORWARD

There are mysteries in the world that are almost impossible to imagine. People find it hard to believe in a great many things yet there are those that devote themselves to the study of proving the impossible can be possible. Archaeologists, anthropologists, scientists, doctors, and other experts in many areas dedicate their lives to research and study to help bring the world to further understanding of teaching that the world is a much bigger place than what is seen in plain view. The study of the supernatural and paranormal are such areas of study.

One of the most explored fields of the supernatural is in the area of angels. The heavenly beings that make up both light and dark forces that interact with humanity is a topic that has been ever present since the very beginning when people first laid eyes on a being that didn't appear human. To identify an angel in the physical realm is a very rare occurrence, but it has been documented as happening over and over. People in modern times have witnessed beings they thought of as angels appearing as both male and female. From a biblical perspective, there is evidence that angels have appeared as males in the times they have been seen by mankind. There is also evidence of angels being seen in the female form or, to be more specific, as women.

The research in this book is based on evidence found in scripture to help identify angels in the female form through three areas of literal identification by physical description, words and phrases such as bird and group names that identify angels as angelic beings rather than as an animal or human, and historical accounts spread throughout the Bible and other cultural references. Other areas that will be covered are ancient cultures and religions viewing of female goddesses, spirits, and demons, the study of the duality of why an angel appears either male or female, and the study of such areas of witch craft, the influence of spirits on people through the occult, and the impact of negative and positive spirits physically, psychologically, and spiritually.

The purpose for this book is to further reveal all the mysteries of the Bible. While a controversial subject for many readers, the evidence that will be presented in this book is based on careful study of scripture from English, Hebrew, and Greek texts, words, and definitions. Further research was done in cultural identification from the Middle East, Levant, and Jewish civilizations, which explored the possibility of women angels. An application of various fields of psychology has also been used to help educate the readers on what can occur with male and female angels, spirits, and demons.

Angels don't have a gender in the traditional sense of male and female. Angels appear as men or women in the physical realm, in visions, and in dreams for certain representations that call for the use of appearing as a particular gender for specific reasons. They can take other forms such as animals and even natural elements. Being that they can appear in physical form, angels can interact with humans, nature, and other areas of existence. Some have even had sexual relations with humans to produce offspring at certain times in the Bible and history.

Other subjects that will be included in this book will cover several areas that are heavily influenced by the spiritual realm. Topics that will be included are on addiction, feminism, duality, impacts of current world events, magic, and other areas that angels, spirits, and demons take an interest in for various purposes. The subjects outlined in the following chapters will help the reader learn to see the world, the supernatural, God, and the Bible in ways that are unique. This book will reveal things never before examined or thought about, until now.

CHAPTER 1: WINGS OF BIRDS

The very first thing to use to identify a female angel in Biblical scripture is actual scripture. The most widely used scripture in existence on identifying female angels is found in the book of Zechariah. Zechariah 5:9 KJV says, *"Then I lifted up mine eyes, and looked, and behold, there came out two women, and the wind was in their wings; for they had wings like the wings of a stork: and they lifted up the ephah (basket or measurement such as a weight) between the earth and heaven."*

The book of Zechariah was by a Jewish prophet during the Babylonian captivity. Zechariah witnessed first hand imagery of angels that were far different than previous accounts. His description of seeing women with wings like that of storks as opposed to seeing angels that look like men is the first literal description of physical differences between male and female angels.

Male angels in the Bible go by many names. A group of male angels are sometimes called the sons of God, or in Hebrew the *Bene Elohim*. The female equivalent in Hebrew is the *Hbnvt Shl Lyhym* (Elohim) meaning daughters of God. The question is how to identify female angels in the Bible? The beginning to such knowledge is to understand that not all words in the Bible are what they seem to represent. Like the Hebrew words that mean sons and daughters of God, there are particular words and translations of words that, even if they look like they represent something, they actually might refer to something else.

Hebrew and Greek words often have multiple definitions. Take the Hebrew word *'nesher'* as an example of a word with a double meaning. The word nesher means vulture in one definition, and eagle in another meaning of the word. The double definition of the word 'nesher' is one example of how to identify angels in the Bible as many spiritual beings, both angelic and fallen, are identified with bird symbols.

Exodus 19:4 ESV uses an interesting reference to an eagle as it reads, *"You yourselves have seen what I did to the Egyptians, and how I bore you on eagles' wings and brought you to myself."* The reference to being mounted on wings of eagles is not necessarily referencing an eagle as a bird, but deliverance.

Ecclesiastes 10:20 NRSV says, *"Do not curse the king, even in your thoughts, or curse the rich, even in your bedroom; for a bird of the air may carry your voice, or some winged creature tell the matter."*

Scripture often maintains a reference to an angelic or spiritual being using terms such as bird, star, or host. Bird terminology is often one of the more widely used identifications associated with angels used in the Bible. There are two ways that angels are identified with birds.

Angels are sometimes referenced with particular species of birds. The relationship between angels and birds is based on two specific points of identification. The first would be when an angel is identified as an angel with a particular kind of bird wings. The second is when the name of an actual bird is used in place of the word angel. Using the Zechariah 5:9 description of women angels with wings of storks is the most vivid of seeing an angel not as a man, but as a woman. The female angels identified by physical description are further identified with the wings of a stork.

Another set of scriptures that goes unnoticed is in Psalms 68:12-13 KJV, *"Kings of armies did flee apace: and she that tarried at home divided the spoil. Though ye have lien among the pots, yet shall ye be as the wings of a dove covered with silver, and her feathers with yellow gold."* Psalms uses many poetic descriptions in its vocabulary. However, Psalms is not singularly poetic. The physical descriptions found in the book of Psalms are often based in truths of people, places, or things that have been witnessed by the authors.

Revelation 12:14 KJV reads, *"And to the woman were given two wings of a great eagle, that she might fly into the wilderness, into her place, where she is nourished for a time, and times, and half a time, from the face of the serpent."* This scripture and Psalms 68:12-13 verses give two descriptions possible of women angels. One is that the scriptures describe women with bird wings similar to the female angels mentioned in Zechariah 5:9. The second description is that the women are representing particular spiritual fulfillment duties carried out with a specific function and purpose. Such types of tasks are associated with paragons.

The word paragon is defined as a person of preeminent qualities that acts as a model or pattern of some given quality. Each of the three descriptions of women angels or women with bird wings in the books of Zechariah, Psalms, and Revelation give account for a particular task that is carried out by characters with preeminent qualities that are lined up for a specific outcome. The books of Zechariah and Revelation are prophetic books, and the women carry out future tasks.

Psalms is not a book of pure prophecy like Zechariah or Revelation. It does however contain some predictions of future events. The main observation in terms of lessons found in Psalms is to deal with spiritual, ethical, and moral instructions and directions. Psalms is also filled with beautiful words of poetry.

Each bird used in the three scriptures from Zechariah, Psalms, and Revelation are animals of particularly distinguishing characters. The stork is identified as a baby-bringer or bringer of life due to it being a water bird and water is a symbol of life. A stork is identified as a feminine symbol of creation, renewal, and rebirth. In the ancient world the symbol of water was significant as it represented the womb or creation of life.

White Stork (top) courtesy of Carlos Delgado. Golden Eagle (bottom left) courtesy of Tony Hisgett. Laughing Dove (bottom right) courtesy of Lip Kee.

When taking a closer look at the scriptures following Zechariah 5:9, we read Zechariah 5:10, 11 KJV, *"Then I said to the angel that talked with me, whither do these (the women with stork wings) bear the epah?[1] And he said unto me, to build it an house in the land of Shinar: and it shall be established, and set there upon her own base."* The epah or measurement is a representation of the

---

[1] Author' note in parentheses.

spirit of wickedness that is to be built up in Shinar or Babylon. The scriptural wording of "to build" and "shall be established" sets up perfectly parallel to the women who are represented with stork wings as they create by building up a house to contain the epah and the wickedness.

The Psalms 68:12-13 scripture of women with doves wings of silver and feathers of yellow gold also yield an important meaning. Doves symbolize love, peace, and messengers. Silver is associated with symbols of ornate, glamour, graceful, sophisticated, and elegant. The meaning of gold is illumination, wealth, and wisdom. Another symbol gold represents is "high quality."[2] The accompanying scripture to Psalms 68:12-13 is seen in Psalms 68:10-11 ESV give the parallel to the symbolism of the doves as they read, *"Your flock found a dwelling in it; in your goodness, O God, you provided for the needy. The Lord gives the Word; the women who announce the news are a great host."*

In some translations of the Bible the word women is replaced with army as is common with different translations of the Bible. In the representation, the dove wings, silver, and feathers of gold are aligned with peace, abundance of wealth from the spoils or bounty taken from the armies that fled, and the highest quality of goods that were divided among the spoils of the enemy.

---

[2] Gold represents compassion, illumination, love, courage, passion, wisdom, grandeur, prosperity, wealth, and glamour, success, and extravagance.

Revelation 12:14 gives a vision of a bird that is a very common figure of power in the ancient and the modern world. The eagle is associated with symbols of great strength, vision, leadership, warlike ferocity, dominion, nobility, victory, and timing. The use of the eagle's wings with the woman fleeing into the wilderness for an appointed time and was nourished in "her place" for a time from the face of the serpent line up with the eagle as a symbol of timing, vision, and great strength.

Each bird representation from the aforementioned female

angels or spirits lines up angels and their roles as listed in three scriptures. First in Hebrews 1:14 ESV, *"Are they not all ministering spirits sent out to serve for the sake of those who are to inherit salvation?"* Then in Colossians 1:16 ESV, *"For by Him all things were created, in heaven and on earth, visible and invisible, whether thrones or dominions or rulers or authorities-all things were created through Him for Him."* Lastly in Psalm 91:11 ESV, *"For He will command His angels concerning you to guard you in all your ways."* Due to the fact that each of these scriptures has to do with a particular purpose involving mankind, prophecy, or both, we see that each representation of angels and birds fits a particular theme to be fulfilled in the verses listed, then further learned by the readers who are reading them for their own purposes and individual pursuits.

Another interesting bird that is mentioned in the Bible is the mythical Phoenix. Job 29:18 NRSV says, *"Then I thought, 'I shall die in my nest, and I shall multiply my days like the phoenix."* The New Revised Standard Version uses the name phoenix in the Job scripture, while the King James Version uses the word sand in its place. Both words come from the Hebrew word *chol.* Chol (also pronounced hol) is used to define sand, palm tree, and phoenix in Hebrew. The Hebrew word *Milcham* is also used to identify a phoenix.

The Phoenix bird comes from ancient Egypt. There it is known as the *Bennu.* It is that said that the Bennu dwelled in the land where modern day Saudi Arabia is situated. It is a bird that represents death and rebirth after burning up every 500 years into ashes, and then is reborn from those ashes. Ashes are unique among Jews and Christians as they can represent "dust." Mankind was made from the dust of the earth, and returns to it at death as read in Genesis 3:19. This brings to mind the old expression of, "Ashes to ashes, dust to dust." The wording of dust and ash comes together in Job 30:19 ESV that states, *"God has cast me into the mire, and I have become like dust and ashes."* Dust and ashes appear as the same thing in the eyes of Jewish belief and symbolism.

Ashes and dust represent a type of purifying force in the ancient world. Mourners and sinners would put ash or dust (seen sometimes as the same thing) on their heads to represent atonement, repentance, and purification. Ashes were used in Jewish temple sacrifices for the atonement of sin. Some examples of this were the spreading of ashes from a Red Heifer after it was sacrificed and burned. Ashes that were spread over a slaughtered fowl from a sacrifice. Also, the gathering up of ashes by a clean man was used for rituals of atonement and purification.

Ecclesiastes 12:7 ESV says, *"And the dust returns to the earth as it was, and the spirit returns to God who gave it."* Ashes represent dust, and dust represents earth. Mankind does indeed die, and their bodies return to the dust of the earth. But, their spirit can live on in eternal life with God when they receive His gift of salvation.

The phoenix bird is used as a representation of death and rebirth. This is an example of eternal life. Many early church Christians used the phoenix as a symbol to represent the death and resurrection of Jesus. A Phoenix is described as looking like an eagle with wings of fire and gold. Whether real, an angel, or something else, the finding of a phoenix in the Bible is a testament to the role of birds in the word of God. In the next chapter will be an examination of the secondary specifics of identification with angels and birds. The next identifying point is when an angel is referenced as a particular type of bird. Such a labeling with bird names is used for angelic hosts, demonic entities, and particular spirits.

CHAPTER 2: BIRDS AS ANGELS, ANGELS AS BIRDS

There are several ways to identify angels in scripture. Some angels are seen in human form. Some are seen with wondrous features such as wings, multiple heads, or even without form such as the "Ophanim" or wheels within wheels as described in Ezekiel 1:15-21. Others are sometimes seen in the forms of animals similar to how the Holy Spirit was witnessed being seen in the form of a dove when He came to Christ following his baptism in Matthew 3:16 ESV, *"And when Jesus was baptized, immediately He went up from the water, and behold, the heavens were opened to Him, and He saw the Spirit of God descending like a dove and coming to rest on Him."*

Angels can be seen as males or females with animal like traits. On rare occasions angels can be viewed in their divine forms such as when the Minor Prophets were allowed to see the angels of the Ophanim (Ezekiel 1:15-21), Seraphim (Isaiah 6:2), and the Four Living Creatures that surrounded the throne of God (Revelation 4:6).[3] One other way angels can be identified in appearance is in the form of animals. The evidence presented in scripture is a combination of bird and mammals with birds being the more dominant creatures identified with angels.

Bird symbols are among the few acceptable artistic images

---

[3] There is a back and forth debate on whether the Four Living Creatures are Cherubim, or their own separate class of angel. Evidence to support the idea of the four living creatures being cherubim are based on the animal and human faces that the four living creatures have as seen in Ezekiel 1:10-11 and Revelation 4:7. Cherubim are often identified with the same traits of a lion, eagle, ox, and human. The NIV and ESV Bibles use the name cherubim in Ezekiel 10:4. Cherubim are even witnessed in a group of four as described in Exodus 25:18-20.

that were allowed for use in early Jewish culture. Deuteronomy 5:8-10 NAS states:

"You shall not make for yourself an idol, or any likeness of what is in heaven above or on the earth or in the water under the earth. You shall not worship them or serve them; for I, the Lord your God, am a jealous God, visiting the iniquity of the fathers on the children, and on the third and the fourth generations of those who hate me, but showing loving kindness, to those who love Me and keep My commandments."

The same commandment is mentioned in Exodus 20:4-6 ESV:

"You shall not make for yourself a carved image, or any likeness of anything that is in heaven above, or that is in the earth beneath, or that is in the water under the earth. You shall not bow down to them or serve them, for I the Lord your God am a jealous God, visiting the iniquity of the fathers on the children to the third and the fourth generation of those who hate me, but showing steadfast love to thousands of those who love me and keep my commandments."

Jewish artists and authors circumvented certain restrictions in their works with the use of bird images to relate metaphors and portrayals of certain characters rather than in forms that would imply deification. Israelites were forbidden to make images of God, but could make images of God's angels such as the cherubim on top and on the sides of the Ark of the Covenant, provided the images were used for a particular function of reverence for God or Yahweh.

Angels represented literally as birds symbolize their exotic, charming, and commanding presence. Each bird stands for a particular function. Angels also can work with birds or command them such as witnessed in Revelation 19:17 ESV, *"Then I saw an angel standing in the sun, and with a loud voice he called to all the birds that fly directly overhead, "come gather for the great supper of God."* Such visualization is done for teachings, lessons, and knowledge that is identified with each character associated with each lesson or knowledge present. Such views can be seen with the use of male and female angels. Women angels portray an opposite nature to male angels. The opposing nature is not an alternative state, but a duality of male/female representation.

Opposite nature used in male and female roles is not to say that they are in opposition to each other, but rather to represent opposing viewpoints. Think of it as the head and tail of a coin. Both sides are apart of the same coin, but represent two different natures. Male and female angelic figures can represent the same theme, but in a completely opposite way. What this means is that a particular lesson or story the Bible teaches may be witnessed in ways not opposite of each other, but parallel or side by side to each other.

The Hebrew and Arabic word for angel is Malach. Malach is the male pronunciation for angel with Malacha being the female equivalent. The linguistic application of male and female pronunciation is vital in the every day living of the Arab and Jewish worlds. In Middle East tradition, male and female roles are everything. While angels are not as inhibited as human beings, they do manifest in ways that imply correct roles for their purposes.

It is important to understand duality when studying male and female angels and spirits. The underlying reason is to see why angels appear in male or female form. In the Bible, it is

BALANCE = CORRECT

PERFECTION
=
C
O
R
RIGHT   R   WRONG
E
C
T
=
EXCELLENCE

*Chart Of The Correct Balance Between Right and Wrong.

the male equivalent that is often witnessed interacting with humanity. However, given greater attention to detail the appearing of women angels can be made more apparent. Bird symbolism is one way to see them as they represent a particular theme opposite of what male angels normally represent. It is a matter of correct balance for a spirit of excellence.

Titus 2:3-5 ESV gives an interesting account, and is set apart from many other scriptures on the role of women:

"Older women likewise are to be reverent in behavior, not slanderers or slaves to much wine. They are to teach what is good, and so train the young women to love their husbands and children, to be self-controlled, pure, working at home, kind, and submissive to their own husbands, that the word of God may not be reviled."

Let me be clear that I see women as more that just people that need to be married and submissive to a husband. I see women as equal to men in life. The women in my life have always been strong, independent, smart, and loyal people that did amazing things with their lives, yet were also wonderful mothers, wives, businesswomen, and friends.

The Biblical scriptures that talk about women were written by individuals that were raised in times that saw the roles of women differently than modern times. While some scriptures basically lowered women's status, many scriptures sought to raise them to levels of greatness. In the case of the Titus scripture it is not the role of women as wives and mothers that is important, but the character of a woman that matters to the subject at hand.

Women and birds share many similar traits. It is this similarity that is perhaps why women angels are identified as and with birds in the Bible. How do we separate actual birds from angels as birds in scripture? The answer lies in the wording in various languages other than English and the roles used to describe birds of the 66 books of the Bible.

Hebrew and Greek are among the most complicated languages in the world both in their ancient and modern tongues. Both languages were used to make up the Old and New Testaments. Each uses words that have double to triple definitions that may make a reader wonder why such a word was used for a particular scripture. Hebrew words for birds can identify two species of bird with one word such as the name in Hebrew *nesher*. Nesher can mean eagle and vulture. Another Hebrew word *oreb* means both raven and crow.

Many rabbis and scholars often argue over the actual meaning of the words used to describe animals and other things in the Bible as simply meaning one thing rather than something else. The truth however is that each word is interchangeable. Therefore, it is that reason so many times, that a particular word is used in a specific function making the word confusing. Hebrew words for both angels and birds share this common problem of grammatical identification and definition.

How do birds represent angels? The representation is done through what a particular bird represents. Let us look at the properties of the vulture and the eagle. In the Jewish viewpoints of these birds are found identifying traits that lay out markers for seeing an angel or an actual bird being represented in Biblical narratives. English translations are difficult to apply to such a study, as there are many different Biblical translations. It is not impossible with English, but requires a certain level of application of linguistics and translation. What needs to be applied for a proper tool is the correct interpretation of the Biblical narrative through the actual meaning of the words and names found in the Bible.

The first example of bird names we will look at is symbols of death. Matthew 24:28 ESV says, *"For wherever the corpse is, there the vultures will gather."* The same wording is used again in Luke 17:37 ESV which reads, *"And they said to Him, 'Where*

Group of White Backed Vultures Over a Carcass Courtesy of
Magnus Kjaergaard.

Lord?" He said to them, "Where the corpse is, there the vultures will gather." The word eagle is used in the King James Version of the Bible, but eagle and vulture are interchangeable due to the original Hebrew word *nesher*.

It needs to be pointed out that while the word nesher does mean vulture and eagle, many translators of the Bible got the meaning incorrect when they mixed eagle up with vulture as the original Hebrew meaning of nesher was vulture. The identity of an eagle came from the Greek word *a'eotos*, which means eagle. The Orthodox Jewish Bible uses the word nesher meaning vulture for both the Old and New Testament. Another word for nesher in Hebrew is nesharim.

Symbols of death in Jewish and Christian tradition are done with birds such as vultures, crows, ravens, owls, and the ostrich. Each bird represents a particular image of scavengers that feeds off corpses, occupies areas of desolation and destruction, and are carriers of omens of death as they will circle over or linger near the dead and dying.

Psalm 23: 4 ESV says, *"Even though I walk through the valley of the shadow of death, I will fear no evil, for you are with me; your rod and your staff, they comfort me."* The mention of the valley of the shadow of death is of interest as such a place is what a battlefield is considered due to the amount of death brought forth in battle.

2 Corinthians 4:17-18 ESV states:

"For this light momentary affliction is preparing for us an eternal weight of glory beyond all comparison, as we look not to the things that are seen but to the things that are unseen. For the things that are seen are transient, but the things that are unseen are eternal."

Battle and death are a form of affliction. Death is a substance that God will throw into the Lake of Fire at the end of days. The most fascinating aspect of the valley of the shadow of death is that there are several places mentioned in the Bible and throughout the world that share that title. These places are said to be where spirits dwell and occupy. One such creature is the screech owl.

Isaiah 34:14 KJV says, *"The wild beasts of the desert shall also meet with the wild beasts of the island, and the satyr shall cry to his fellow; the screech owl also shall rest there, and find for herself a place of rest."*

In the Jewish Orthodox Bible and the *Tanakh* or Hebrew Bible, the screech owl is called Lilit or Lilith. Lilith is a demonic creature that Jewish views have identified as a demon of the night, stealer of babies in the darkness, and is identified with the screech owl. Lilith is mentioned in proto-Semitic (also called proto-Hebrew) as a disease bearing wind spirit. She is identified with wings in certain ancient depictions from Babylonian and Mesopotamian art and stone work that are similar to the descriptions of women angels seen in Zechariah 5:9. While not a representation of death, the mention of her finding a place of rest coincides with another scripture found in Isaiah 34:11 KJV, *"But the cormorant and the bittern shall possess it; the owl and the raven shall dwell in it: and He shall stretch out upon it the line of confusion, and the stones of emptiness."*

These scriptures of Isaiah 34:11 and 34:14 are apart of a theme of battle, slaughter, and desolation that make up the whole of the 34th chapter of Isaiah. The mention of the raven is of particular note as the raven or Orev (Oreb) is considered a death bird and symbol of death in Jewish belief. Oreb is a dual meaning word that can be applied to both a raven and a crow. The identification of Lilith as a screech owl is one example of a different translation of a bird taking the place of an angel, spirit, or demon. A fact that is further made is that the screech owl is identified as a female spirit or demon and thus giving proof in the Bible of angels and other spirits, female included, as birds.

29

Aside from birds as being identified as angels, another identifying marker is actual elements. One example found in scripture is the counterpart to Lilith that is found in Genesis 14:14. She is known as Laila or Layla.[4] Layla is identified with night similar to Lilith, but in the service of God rather than for demonic considerations. The next chapter will explore the use of elemental spirits and what they represent in scripture.

---

[4] Identified by the name Layla in the Orthodox Jewish Bible.

CHAPTER 3: ELEMENTS AND SPIRITS

The book of Job is one of the books of the Bible that produces unique imagery of angels and spirits. One scripture that is of particular interest is seen in Job 30:8. This single scripture lists an interesting point of observation. Job 30:8 KJV says, *"They were children of fools, yea, children of base men: they were viler than the earth."* What makes this scripture stand out is the use of 'children being viler than the earth.'

The wording of Job 30:8 in the King James Version is listed quite differently in other translations. Other Biblical translations such as the English Standard Version has the scripture of Job 30:8 say, *"A senseless brood, they have been whipped from the land."* Many new translations follow a similar sentence structure of talking about people being expelled from the land, but the KJV version of the Bible speaks in a way that could define the earth in a manner representing a spiritual manifestation.

Most people would assume that angels are either spiritual beings that have the form of a humanlike appearance with wings, or can appear as humans that walk and talk with mankind. Both of these types of descriptions are listed in scripture. However, the imagery of angelic beings is not limited to simple humanlike beings and even creatures with human or animal like features. Some angels and spirits can actually be manifested in nature itself as primordial substances, and even natural phenomena such as the literal manifestation of *night* (or darkness).

Many readers will ask the question of where exactly in scripture is such descriptions of angels being seen as natural

10th-Century Paris Psalter of Isaiah (Right) and The Greek Elemental Night Goddess Nyx (Left) Who Is Similar to Lailah. Courtesy of Neuceu.

phenomena and natural substances found? First, let us cover classifications of angels and spirits that take those of both light and dark to much more expanded roles. There are several scriptures that list the different kinds of angelic classes, but what makes certain scriptures standout are specific words used for particular angels or in this case elemental spirits.

1 Peter 3:22 NIV says, *"Who has gone into heaven and is at God's right hand with angels, authorities and powers in submission to Him."* Ephesians 1:21 KJV reads, *"Far above all principality, and power, and might, and dominion, and every name that is named, not only in this world, but also in that which is to come."* Then in Ephesians 6:12 KJV it states, *"For we wrestle not against flesh and blood, but against principalities, against powers, against rulers of darkness of this world, against spiritual wickedness in high places."* Each of these scriptures identifies supernatural forces of powers, dominions, principalities, authorities, and might. While the scriptures do list other titles, it is the words that describe forces that may not refer to individual's that may be seen in a physical form.

Colossians 2:8 ESV reads, *"See to it that no one takes you captive by philosophy and empty deceit, according to human tradition, according to the elemental spirits of the world, and not according to Christ.* Colossians 2:20 ESV states, *"If with Christ you died to the elemental spirits of the world, why, as if you were still alive in the world, do you submit to regulations."* We see the term *elemental spirits* used in the Colossian scriptures. Worded in a similar yet different manner, Galatians 4:3 ESV reads, *"In the same way we also, when we were children, were enslaved to the elementary principles of the world."* Elemental spirits and elementary principles in these scriptures represent the same concept of spirits that are of a more primordial representation in identification and function.

2 Peter 2:11 KJV reads, *"Whereas angels, which are greater in power and might, bring not railing accusation against them before the Lord."* Angels are beings of incredible power and abilities. With the scriptures of Colossians, Galatians, and Job we can see that there are angels, which make up elements and rudiments of nature itself. The word rudiment is defined as an elementary or primitive form of something. If we look at the root of *principality* we would get the word *principle*. Principle is defined as a fundamental source or basis of something. Just like humanity has its roots in the very dust of the earth, angels also have their beginnings that have a primordial essence.

There is a difference between the natural source of dust that man descends from and the source of life from which angels come. Angels are not like God the Father, the Son, and the Holy Spirit. The Trinity as the God Head is referred to was in existence before even light was created. Angels were beings created into existence sometime in the early creation of the cosmos and rudimentary elements of life. Genesis 2:1 KJV says, *"Thus the heavens and the earth were finished, and all the host of them."* The Genesis 2:1 scripture uses the term *host*. Host is identified both with angels, stars, planets, and other celestial bodies of space. It is very possible that the identity of host in Genesis 2:1 refers to forms of angelic and cosmological entities together. The most likely time that angels came into existence prior to Genesis 2:1 would be in the first chapter of Genesis between verses 2 and 4. Some scholars have referred to that theory as the "Gap

Theory."

The verses between Genesis 1:2-4 deal with the creation of light, darkness, chaos, goodness, earth, and water. The King James Bible uses the word *deep* in verse 2. Deep is defined as 'extending far down from the top or surface or deeply' into something. There is a literary meaning of the word deep that means 'very intense or extreme.' There is even a nautical definition of "deep" that stands for the denizens (inhabitant of a particular place) of the (deep) sea. What could the term "deep" actually mean though when identified in terms of primordial matters?

There is mention of 'the deep' in the book of Proverbs. Proverbs 8:27 ESV states, *"When He established the heavens, I was there; when He drew a circle on the face of the deep..."* The deep described in the Proverbs scripture is in reference to '"without form and void" that was over the face of the deep at the time of creation. This description comes from Genesis 1:2 where not even light was in existence until God created it (or declared it into existence) in Genesis 1:3.

Genesis 1:2 KJV states, *"And the earth was without form, and void; and darkness was upon the face of the deep. And the Spirit of God moved upon the face of the waters."* The word deep in the Bible comes from the Hebrew word *tehom*. The word tehom represents the same meaning as the Greek word *abyssos*.

Abyssos means abyss in the English translation. While some people may define abyss in the Biblical sense as a representation of hell or the grave, the definition for abyss or deep in terms of the beginnings of existence is the great deep of the primordial waters of creation. The Hebrew word tehom shares similar meaning with the Akkadian word *tamtu* and the Ugaritic *thm*. This is pointed out to show the connections that Hebrew as a language has to other Semitic and Levantine languages.

It is important to understand that many of the Jewish stories derive from the descendants of Abraham, the people that surrounded them, and from the very people that Abraham descended. Abraham (originally Abram) lived in the land of Ur that is located in modern day Iraq. His people were not Jewish but Semitic. Semitic is a word that is derived from the name of Noah's son Shem. It represented a multitude of ethnic, cultural, racial, and language or linguistic groups from which the Jewish people would descend. Even the modern language term for Semitic represents not only the Hebrew language but also Arabic, Aramaic, Akkadian, Phoenician, and many Afro-Asiatic family languages. Such facts and information is vital to consider when studying the history and culture of God's chosen people to understand who they are, where they come from, and what they represent as a people.

The Levant has cultures that portrayed many angelic and demonic figures both in male and female forms. Hebrew and Arabic languages use the same male and female names for angel or *Malach* (same name in both languages) represented by the male pronunciation form *Malakh,* and the female pronunciation form *Malaika.* Upon closer inspection of the cultural backgrounds, the Hebrew Bible or *Tanakh* uses many

*Ancient of Day Painting By William Blake Depicting God Creating
Life From the Darkness and Giving Life Direction. Courtesy of
Jaybear*

names in places normally reserved for words that represent

*Gaia (Gaea), The Earth, Depicted As a Woman By Anselm
Feuerbach. Courtesy of Salomis.*

objects, events, and natural phenomenon instead of people or animals. The Greeks used a similar approach to the naming of things of nature and natural phenomenon with actual names instead of a standard mark of identification. In Greek mythology many of the primordial beings that created the Titans and gods were given names. They were not gods or Titans, but forces of nature and other aspects of reality such as time and chaos.

The Greeks believed that the Titans, gods, giants, and other primordial creations such as sea gods came from primordial deities that represented earth, sky, Tartarus (a type of maximum security prison in Hell) or abyss, mountains, darkness, chaos, sea, night, light, and day. It is from these natural elements that other sentient life would rise. One fascinating point of observation is that many of the primordial Greek deities have dual representations as both male and female. Such representation is called *dualism*.

Dualism is defined as the state of two parts. It denotes co-eternal binary opposition which is a pair of related terms or concepts that are opposite in meaning and set off against one another. Another view of dualism in terms of metaphysical and philosophical duality usages is to indicate a system, which contains two essential parts. Dualism can be seen in an example of benevolent versus malevolent or two moral opposites at work. The elements that make up mankind can be viewed the same way.

In the 1995 superhero movie *Tank Girl,* the main villain and owner of a company called Water & Power Corporation named Kesslee (played by Malcolm McDowell) said, "Adam was dust until God injected him with life, and do you know what was in that injection? It was water. Water is life and water is power." Scripture tells us that God formed man out of the dust of the earth, but breathed into man to give him life. However, an argument can be made that the breath of God could have been water. II Peter 3:5 ESV reads, *"But they deliberately forget that long ago by God's word the heavens came into being and the earth was formed out of water and by water."*

If one were to look closely at the ingredients that make up a human body, 60% of the body of a man is made up of water. There is only 50% of water found in the body of a woman. The human body contains many salts with the majority being sodium. Sodium is essential as a nutrient in humans. It is not reproduced in the human body, so it must be replenished whenever possible.

Sodium is vital as it regulates many bodily functions. It is contained in body fluids that transport oxygen and nutrients. Sodium also maintains the bodies overall fluid balance. Without sodium, the human bodies' senses would dull and the nerves would not function.

Chlorine is the other most important salt in the body. Chlorine equals out to .15% (sodium is also equaled out to .15%) of the salt percentage in the human body. The amount of salt in human blood is .9%. Other elements that make up the human body that are found in the earth is calcium, potassium, sulfur, magnesium, iron, zinc, fluorine, copper, iodine, selenium, chromium, manganese, cobalt, and a few other essential materials for a good and healthy body. In Genesis 2:7, God formed man from the dust of the ground. Dust in the modern day scientific definition is made up of all kinds of particles, but most especially soil. Simple soil is naturally occurring mixtures of mineral and organic ingredients that contain form, composition, and structure. Soil contains the exact same ingredients (most soil anyway) that make up the average human body. Soil also contains 25% water. So, when God formed man out of the dust of the earth, He also used water to balance out the body of what would become human beings.

Why is this important to mention? Most people never realize that just like salt water, regular drinking water also contains salt or at least 9 grams of sodium. A substance such as water that is normally seen as a pure liquid contains a solid material in its material makeup. As made evident in II Peter 3:5, water and earth share a nature of dualism called Monism.

Monism is defined in two ways that are both a wide view and a restricted view. The wide view definition of monism is that something is monistic if is it postulates unity of origin of all things; all things that exist return to a source that is distinct from them. Genesis 3:19 ESV states, *"By the sweat of your face you shall eat bread, till you return to the ground, for out of it you were taken; for you are dust, and to the dust you shall return."* When humans die, they return to the source that they were made from in the beginning. The more restricted definition states that something requires not only unity of origin, but also unity of substance and essence. Leviticus 2:13 ESV says, *"You shall season all your grain offerings with salt. You shall not let the salt of the covenant with your God be missing from your grain offering; with all your offerings you shall offer salt."*

Salt is an essential part of offerings to God. The term "salt of the covenant" represents a binding element that keeps a solemn promise between man and God. Matthew 5:13 ESV reads, *"You are the salt of the earth, but if salt has lost its taste, how shall its saltiness be restored? It is no longer good for anything except to be thrown out and trampled under people's feet."* Just like salt, humans can lose their flavor, become corrupted, and then must be removed from the equation. The same can be said of the nature of life itself.

All things have a balance to it. One thing works together or against something else in order for a cycle of existence to continue. Concepts such as nature or the essence of nature, freewill, and even sin all have a never-ending cycle to them, as they are choices and formless states of being. Death is not considered into these things however as death itself has what freewill, nature, and sin don't have which is an *end.*

Revelation 20:14 ESV says, *"Then Death and Hades were thrown into the lake of fire. The lake of fire is the second death."* Mankind allowed death to enter into the world when humanity fell in the Garden of Eden where God warned about death upon eating of the Tree of Knowledge of Good and Evil. Genesis 2:17 ESV reads, *"But you must not eat from the tree of the knowledge of good and evil, for when you eat from it you will certainly die."*

Whether death was present in the animal or plant kingdoms in the very beginning can't be fully confirmed. Though, one would suspect it was due to the nature of animals and plants needing to eat each other for survival that death perhaps was presented in the animal kingdom. What can be said is mankind brought death upon them when they embraced the fruit of the tree and their disobedience to God.

II Chronicles 13:5 ESV states, *"Ought you not to know that the Lord God of Israel gave the kingship over Israel forever to David and his sons by a covenant of salt?"* Salt was what established the covenant between the line of David and the eventual rise of Jesus as the Messiah to Israel. Mark 9:50 ESV reads, *"Salt is good, but if salt has lost its saltiness, how will you make it salty again? Have salt in yourselves, and be at peace with one another."*

Another interesting scripture that comes before Mark 9:50 is Mark 9:49 ESV that says, *"For everyone will be salted with fire."* Fire is often looked at as something to be feared such as when one thinks about the fires of Hell or the Lake of Fire. However, fire is also something to be revered, as fire is a purifier. God Himself is called an all-consuming fire in Hebrew 12:19. God is the greatest purifying force, and thus makes fire something that is pure and holy.

Salt can purify water in its chlorine form. Chlorine can kill disease-causing pathogens in water such as bacteria, protozoans, and viruses that grow in water supplies. Chlorine can act as an effective disinfectant for water and can thus be drinkable in tap water making it appear acceptable as a part of water, which is a giver of life.

Water purifies by washing away filth and dirt. All of the elements mentioned of earth, water, fire, and even air are purifying and life giving forces. Air is a life giving force as Genesis 7:22 ESV states, *"Everything on the dry land in whose nostrils was the breath of life died."* This is further evidenced in Ezekiel 37:5 ESV as it reads, *"Thus says the Lord God these bones: Behold, I will cause breath to enter you, and you shall live."*

Breath is air that is brought in and out of the body. The elements of earth, air, fire, and water that God made are what can be considered primordial materials that are the purest and therefore make the greatest agents of cleansing, binding, and giving of life that God has made. It is with such an understanding that one can see how God appointed an angel or spirit to have dominion over such elements.

When looking at scripture in the ways of seeing that the angels of God have a role that includes being dominant or having dominion in nature, then one gains a vastly deeper grasp of the infinite realm of the supernatural that God has designed. It also allows people to better understand the dualism that plays into each and every spiritual mentality and being that works with the world around them in the balance between light and dark. Each spirit or angel that is of God or who has fallen carries with it a role or position that is very specific in function.

An interesting question that comes to mind concerning elemental spirits is this. Does the Bible list an angel of a particular element, function, or purpose that is not normally seen in the hierarchy of angels? Another question that seems relevant here, are there only male or are there female angels that have roles with elements? The answer to both questions simultaneously is yes! Yes, there is an angel listed who has a role dealing with an element, and yes there is a female angel listed in such a role instead of just a male counterpart.

Genesis 14:14 speaks of a moment in a battle that Abraham is about to wage to rescue his nephew Lot and his family. Genesis 14:15 ESV reads, *"And He divided his forces against them by night, he and his servants, and defeated them and pursued them to Hobah, north of Damascus."* In the KJV version Genesis 14:15 says, *"And he divided himself against them, by night, and smote them, and pursued them unto Hobah, which is on the left hand of Damascus.*" It is the word *night* that denotes special emphasis here.

The Hebrew translation of the word for night is actually a name known as *Lailah*. The Orthodox Jewish Bible or OJB version of Genesis or Bereshis 14:15 reads, "*And he divided himself against them, he and his avadim, by Lailah, and routed them, and pursued them as far as Chovah, which is on the left hand (north) of Damascus.*" The Orthodox Jewish Bible verse lists the left hand and its north direction for Hobah or Chovah, as well as the English and Hebrew words for proper understanding of translation of scripture for non-Hebrew readers. The JPS or Jewish Publication Society of America Version of the Tanakh (Hebrew Bible or Old Testament) goes further in translation of scripture by identifying Lailah as "an angel called night."

The noun for the word *night* is derived from the Semitic languages with a tri-consonant root spelled L-Y-L. The Arabic word for night is also pronounced *Laylah* due to the Arabic language deriving from Hebrew in origin. The root of Lailah is also shared with the Hebrew word *Lilyt* or Lilith in English translation. The end spelling of Lailah or *lah* sound is feminine. It is one of the few female angel names listed in the Bible that is both a female name, and contains distinct female characteristics. While there is debate as to whether or not Lailah is an actual angel or not, the mention of her in the Jewish Bible and in translations does give rise to a good argument as to her identity as both an elemental spirit and female angel.

Night is defined as the period of time between sunset and sunrise when the sun is below the horizon. Night is considered a part of time. Time is not an element per technical definition, but rather a dimension. Physics tells us that there exist four separate dimensions, which are up and down, back and forth, left and right, and space-time. Space-time is not only a dimension, but also a part of space.

Space and time is thus the same thing and can move about in the first 3 mentioned dimensions. Natural beings can also move about in space and time. Elements such as fire and earth are not actually elements like time, but have been accepted as elements by cultures from ancient Greece and China. There exist 72 actual elements on the Periodic Table of Elements. The relevance here is that like other "elements," night can be considered an elemental spirit.

The ancient Greeks, Chinese, and other civilizations believed there were spirits that made up the primordial material of existence. The Bible has indeed made references to such claims that verify God as their creator and apart of His angelic fold. With the mention of Lailah as the angel of night, then there begs the question of how many other female angels are mentioned in the Bible, and what kind of angels are they? The next chapter will explore not only angels, but also demons that are identified with elements, birds, and other material to shed light on where they are found in the books of the Bible.

CHAPTER 4: NIGHT DEMONS & SPIRITS OF SEDUCTION PART 1

The world is filled with tales of alien abductions, sexual attacks, spiritual manipulation, and demonic possessions that occurred at night. All of these tales are not random phenomena that occur by chance. It is likely those people who have had these encounters have opened doors to the supernatural. They could have done so by performing a ritual with witchcraft or some cultic practice, or by another spiritual, psychological, or physical situation that occurred opening to the realm of angels of the supernatural and paranormal.

Angels do interact with all peoples of the world. Most of the world pays attention to only the angels of God that talk to God's people such as Jews and Christians. Such interactions are only the tip of the iceberg. Angels of darkness and light interact with those that are of different faiths and religions all over the world. There is evidence in the Bible of angels interacting with other cultures and individuals who didn't believe in God but in polytheistic faiths.

Some encounters were physical encounters, while others were in dreams, prophecies, or visions, which would fall under the categories of spiritual and psychological encounters. One account in a dream was encountered by King Nebuchadnezzar of the Chaldean Empire in Daniel 4:13 ESV, *"I saw in the visions of my head as I lay in bed, and behold, a watcher, a holy one, came down from heaven."* Nebuchadnezzar had an encounter with a very unique class of angel. The watchers are among some of the most controversial of angels as they interact with mankind not only in dreams, but also in matters of the flesh and matrimony.

Called the *Iyr* (singular) or *Iyrin* (plural) in Hebrew for awake or watchful, the Watchers as they are known in English are a class of angel that watch, guard, and minister. The Iyr are seen in several books of the Bible by name or by description through their interactions and dealings with mankind. Iyrin are considered the angelic parents of the giants or *Nephilim* found in Genesis chapter six. They possibly taught mankind lessons on magic, idols, and other lessons.

The Iryin are referenced as fulfilling roles in service to God and in service to idolatry in the Bible. The Iryin that served idolatry is not always mentioned by name in the Bible, but can be identified by the way they speak or interact with humanity.

One scripture that can identify Iryin without the name watcher is found in Job 4:12-17 KJV which states, *"Now a word was brought to me stealthily; my ear received the whisper of it. Amid thoughts from visions of the night, when deep sleep falls on men, dread came upon me, and trembling, which made all my bones shake. A spirit glided past my face; the hair of my flesh stood up. It stood still, but I could not discern its appearance. A form was before my eyes; there was silence, then I heard a voice: Can mortal man be in the right before God? Can a man be pure before his Maker?"*

The Job 4:12-17 scriptures lay out three key points to identify the spirit that spoke. The first key point is that the spirit was not identified as a male or female. The second is that the spirit appeared during the night. The third and final point is it made an observation about the role of man made in

comparison to God. These three points give rise to the possibility that the spirit that was possibly the night spirit or demon known as Lilith.

Lilith is one of the few female spirits or demons that is mentioned in the Bible by name. She is mentioned in Isaiah 34:14 in several translations as Lilith, Lilit, the night bird, and the screech owl. As mentioned earlier that certain angels are at times identified with birds, Lilith is associated with the screech owl. Lilith is a name in Hebrew that is defined as meaning night demon or simply the essence of night itself. It is very possible that Lilith may be a female variation of an Iryin.

Job 4:18 KJV reads, *"Even in His servants He puts no trust, and His angels He charges with error."* The word error in some translations is replaced with *folly.* Folly is defined as a lack of good sense or foolishness, and as a foolish act, idea, or practice. The word folly is used in conjunction with or to relate to foolishness, foolhardy, stupidity, idiocy, lunacy, madness, rashness, recklessness, imprudence, injudiciousness, irresponsibility, thoughtlessness, indiscretion, and craziness.

The New American Bible translation is one of the Biblical translations that use the name Lilith in the Bible. Isaiah 34:14 NAB states, *"Wildcats shall meet with desert beasts, satyrs shall call to one another; there shall the Lilith repose, and find for herself a place to rest."* The name Lilith is sometimes replaced with the screech owl in some translations as well as night owl, night-spectre, night monster, vampire, night hag, night bird, and night creature. Each one of these types of creatures is an animal or monster associated with death, lust, horror, kidnapping, and scavenging.

Lilith is used today as an icon among witches, wiccans, and other modern occultism practitioners. One reason for her popularity among witches and wiccans is her association as "first mother" due to her being considered among both secular and Jewish religious and mystic circles as the first wife of Adam created at the same time from the dust of the earth. That claim is controversial as there is no real evidence in the Bible save for a few Hebrew words used in Genesis such as *Adamah* in Genesis 1:26-27, 2:7, and Romans 5:12. Adamah makes reference to both male and female humans being born of the dust of the earth at the same time before Eve who came from the rib of Adam.[5] This is only speculation and bears no real accurate footing in truth. However, it is worth mentioning as it is a topic that is studied and discussed in religion and academic fields.

The claim that Lilith is the first wife of Adam is false. However, it could be argued that Lilith is an Iyr or watcher angel. This is due to the Iryin being the main angels that had married and had sex with human beings to produce the Nephilim giants. One interesting question that comes to mind when thinking about angel parentage is if angels can have sex and produce offspring, can they give birth as well?

The idea of an angel having sex with humans is one thing, while the ability to procreate is an entirely different matter. Yet, there is debate over the possibility that the accounts of Lilith give rise to the possibility that angels and demons can give birth the same way as humans.

The Isaiah 34:14 scripture is one part of a much more detailed illustration when looking at pre and post Isaiah 34:14 scriptures. Isaiah 34:12-17 KJV states, *"It's nobles-there is no one*

---

[5] The idea of Eve coming from the rib of Adam is a common misconception. Eve actually came from the fire of man.

there to call it a kingdom, and all its princes shall be nothing. Thorns shall grow over its strongholds, nettles and thistles in its fortresses. It shall be the haunt of Jackals, an abode for ostriches. And wild animals shall meet with hyenas; the wild goat shall cry to his fellow; indeed, there the night bird settles and finds for herself a resting place. There the owls nests and lays and hatches and gathers her young in her shadow; indeed, there the hawks are gathered, each one with her mate. Seek and read from the book of the Lord: Not one of these shall be missing; none shall be without her mate. For the mouth of the Lord has commanded, and his Spirit has gathered them. He has cast the lot for them; his hand has portioned it out to them with the line; they shall possess it forever; from generation to generation they shall dwell in it."

The place being referenced is the nation of Edom.

Edom is an ancient kingdom located in the southern region of modern day Jordan. It was founded by the first son of Isaac who was known as Esau. Esau is described in the Bible as having red hair. The name Edom translates into meaning 'red.' Esau is not a highly favored character in the Bible. Romans 9:13 ESV says, *"As it is written, Jacob I loved, but Esau I hated."* In Malachi 9:13 ESV it states, *"But Esau I have hated. I have laid waste his hill country and left his heritage to jackals of the desert."*

The lineage of the Edomites who descend from Esau share similar disdain according to Malachi 1:1-14 ESV:

"The oracle of the Word of the Lord to Israel by Malachi. "I have loved you," says the Lord. But you say, "How have you loved us?" Is it not Esau Jacob's brother?" declares the Lord. "Yet I have loved Jacob but Esau I have hated. I have laid waste his hill country and left his heritage to jackals of the desert." If Edom says, "we are shattered but

we will rebuild the ruins," the Lord of hosts says, "They may build, but I will tear down, and they will be called 'the wicked country,' and 'the people with whom the Lord is angry forever." You shall say, "Great is the Lord beyond the border of Israel!"

Esau and the Edomites are clearly noted as not favored people by God or the Israelites.

The character of Esau is not one of a great leader, but rather a loathsome scoundrel. This is made evident in Hebrews 12:16-17 ESV that states, *"That no one is sexually immoral or unholy like Esau, who sold his birthright for a single meal. For you know that afterward, when he desired to inherit the blessing, he was rejected, for he found no chance to repent, though he sought it with tears."*

Esau was both a victim and villain according to Hebrews 12:16-17 scriptures and his full story in Genesis 27. Esau was the twin brother of Jacob who would later be known as Israel. He and his brother struggled with each other even before they were born. God said to Esau's and Israel's mother Rebekah that her sons would struggle with each other as two nations. Genesis 25:23 ESV makes this clear as it states, *"And the Lord said to her, "Two nations are in your womb, and two peoples from within you shall be divided; the one shall be stronger than the other, the older shall serve the younger."*

Esau was the older of the twins by being first born. He was a great hunter and worker of the field. He was a polygamist and married two women of Hittite lineage that were not favored. Esau was foolish and made stupid decisions such as when selling his birthright to his brother for some stew.

Esau was a victim in many ways as his mother and brother stole a blessing that his father wanted to give to him. He instead was given a very harsh blessing as Genesis 27:39-40 ESV says, *"Behold, away from the fatness of the earth shall your dwelling be, and away from the dew of heaven on high. By your sword you shall live, and you shall serve your brother; but when you grow restless you shall break his yoke from your neck."*

Due to that blessing and being robbed by his mother and brother Esau hated Jacob and wanted to kill him. Later, Esau would make peace with his brother. He even married the daughter of his victimized uncle, Ishmael, who was removed from his brother and fathers' family years earlier due to a similar issue involving his half brother, his mother, Isaac's mother, and himself.

Esau and Ishmael are victims of abandonment and reviling by their mother and father. Ishmael would go on to become the father of the Arabic people, and Esau would become the father of the Lebanese people who share Arabic bloodlines with Ishmael. Their blessings and prophecies would trickle down into the people of the Middle East of today.

The fathers of the Arabic peoples and nations have an intertwining with resentment towards women. In the eyes of Arabic men, both in religious custom and natural opinion, women are inferior to men. Such contempt plays a part in the rise of the feminine curses that plague Middle East women. Those issues could be argued to be a part of the reasons that link the Isaiah 34:14 scripture of Lilith with the nation of Edom.

Proverbs 2:16-19 gives an interesting twist on women and what can be called the spirit of seduction. Proverbs 2:16-19 KJV states, *"To deliver thee from the strange woman, even from the stranger which flattereth her words: which forsaketh the guide of her youth, and forgetteth the covenant of her God. For her house inclineth unto death, and her paths unto the dead. None that go unto her return again, neither take they hold of the paths of life."*

Ironically, there is a similar comparison of the Proverbs scripture with a verse from the Dead Sea Scrolls referred to as 4Q184 that reads, *"Her gates are gates of death, and from the entrance of the house she sets out towards Sheol. None of those who enter there will ever return, and all who possess her will descend into the pit."* According to scholars and researchers such as Joseph M. Baumgarten and John J. Collins, the scriptures of Proverbs 2:18-19, and the similar verse in the Qumran scroll 4Q184 where the woman who is identified as the seductress is most likely a female demon or demonic spirit.

As mentioned, spirits can be male and female. The duality of male and female depends on three important factors. The first being the actual sex of the person influenced by a spirit. This is important to understand as the physical attributes of emotion; physical attributes such as sex drive, appeal, physical characteristics, mental state, and even natural physiology can and is effected by spiritual influences. The second is the spiritual factors behind the influence of a spirit.

Spiritual influence of outside sources begins with what a person first manifests in their own spirit. The third and final factors would be those of morality and conviction issues. What a person holds important or doesn't, their beliefs or convictions of heart, and other beliefs or desires that could be positive or negative are all important in spiritual influences. Those kinds of spiritual influences can be very powerful.

One such example of moral issues has to do with masculine and feminine principles that have become a major stable in today's age. Negative and positive influences are important in dealing with feminine and masculine spirituality and spirits. They can define the very nature of the spiritual atmospheres of humanity.

CHAPTER 5: NIGHT DEMONS & SPIRITS OF SEDUCTION PART 2

Throughout the ages many people have sought to understand the beings that make up the supernatural realm. Many cults have been formed and centered on the practice of discovering what is hidden behind the veil of the things not seen by the naked eye. The Jewish practice of Kabbalah (aka Jewish mysticism), and the Islamic study of Sufism are examples of religious mysticism that deals with more rudimentary studies of the supernatural.

It is not surprising to see religions mix God or a deity with mysticism as people have been doing such practices for centuries. The question that needs to be asked is what repercussions would result from such mixings? People quite literally have no idea what they are usually getting involved in when they practice mysticism. The Bible warns of such practices for a variety of reasons.

1 Samuel 15:23 NIV states, *"For rebellion is like the sin of divination, and arrogance like the evil of idolatry. Because you have rejected the word of the Lord, He has rejected you as king."* In Leviticus 19:31 NIV we read, *"Do not turn to mediums or seek out spiritists, for you will be defiled by them. I am the Lord your God."*

2 Chronicles 33:6 NIV gives a very detailed account for dealing with the practices of witchcraft and spiritism as it says, *"He sacrificed his children in the fire in the Valley of Ben Hinnom, practiced divination and witchcraft, sought omens, and consulted mediums and spiritists. He did much evil in the eyes of the Lord, arousing His anger."* Messing with the spiritual realm is like juggling live hand grenades with the pins removed. It's

not about if they will explode, but a matter of when they will explode.

Many witch covens and cults use demons and spirits in their rituals. More specifically they use their names for rituals. The depiction of Lilith is used among many wiccans and witches due to her connection as she has special reverence to the practitioners of Wicca. In certain groups Lilith is even worshiped as a goddess that is sometimes referred to as the "first mother" as mentioned earlier.

It needs to be noted that there is a difference between Wicca and witchcraft. Wicca, referred to as pagan witchcraft, is a relatively new age movement. Wicca is a duotheistic religious movement that believes in both a god and a goddess. Wicca is diverse in its roots as it mixes ancient rituals with modern day hermitic motifs. It has theological and ritual practices that identify it more as a religion instead of a cult or witchcraft coven.

Witchcraft or witchery broadly means the practice of and belief in magical skills and abilities exercised by solitary practitioners and groups. Although very similar, Wicca and witchcraft are different and therefore must be identified separately. Both however would fall under the same definition of witchcraft as laid out in Deuteronomy 18:9–12 ESV:

"When you enter the land the Lord your God is giving you, do not learn to imitate the detestable ways of the nations there. Let no one be found among you who sacrifices their son or daughter in the fire, who practices divination or sorcery, interprets omens, engages in witchcraft, or casts spells, or who is a medium or spiritist or who consults the dead. Anyone

who does these things is detestable to the Lord."

It is important to associate a particular religion, spiritual movement, or cult with its own definitions and functions. To simply say one is the same as another can be dangerous when dealing with research of particular subjects or the attempts at saving people from cults and false religions. To identify something incorrectly would no doubt make followers of a particular group hostile and would make the person making the identification look ridiculous and stupid. Pay careful attention to what something is called, what their practices are, and what is worshiped, as it could be the key to saving someone. Another important reason to identify things correctly is to see what kind of spirits are involved in such groups.

The New Age movement deals heavily with influences from spirits. Though the followers themselves rarely use the term, New Age has a following of people believing it to be religious and a spiritual practice involving spirit, mind, and body. New Age is identified as a form of western Esotericism (meaning hidden or unknown knowledge) or western mystery tradition.

One of the stronger emphases in New Age is the belief in holistic (whole) forms of divinity that empower the universe including humans themselves. The follow-up to that view is the belief in a wide-variety of non-human and semi-divine entities that include angels, spirits, and masters who are people that are influenced by the same spirits and angels who give them ancient knowledge and wisdom by a process called channeling.

Channeling or mediumship is done in two ways. One way is through psychics or people called sensitives who talk to spirits and relay what they hear from them. The second way is when someone goes into a trance and allows a "spiritual entity" to 'borrow' their body and talk through them. One physical example of when a person is channeling a spirit through their body is when they begin to have muscular rigidity, fixity of posture, and decreased sensitivity to pain. Such a condition is known as catalepsy and has further symptoms of rigid body and limbs, staying in the same position when moved, no response, loss of muscle control, and slowing down of breathing and other bodily functions.

Catalepsy is a condition associated with many mental disorders and their treatments or side effects of treatments more specifically such as from the treatment of schizophrenia with anti-psychotics. One of the symptoms of cocaine addiction withdrawal is Catalepsy.

It is fascinating when one notices the connection between how a person channeling a spirit and a cocaine addict experiencing withdrawal display the exact same conditions of catalepsy. 1 Peter 2:11 ESV states, *"Beloved, I urge you as sojourners and exiles to abstain from the passions of the flesh, which wage war against your soul."* The allowing of a spirit to take over a human body during channeling is actually the allowing of a spirit to possess the channeler. It is very likely that the reason the possessed body goes into a state of catalepsy is due to the fact that the human body is not meant to be possessed.

The human body is designed to hold the soul that God made fearfully and wonderfully unique for each individual created. The uniqueness of the soul includes a unique individual body that each person is born with. When a spirit, which will be referred to in this moment as an unclean spirit enters a human body, then an unnatural effect has occurred in both the spiritual and physical balance of a person.

Whether possession is by the allowing of a spirit to enter a person, or by acts that are unknown to a person but allow a spirit to come into them, latch onto them, or influence them, the end result will be side effects that manifest in physical ways. The focus of possession by demons and spirits, all of which is referred to as *pneuma,* is what kinds of spirits are being dealt with when such events occur.

While many spirits that are dealt with by psychics and other New Age people, another spirit that is involved is a spirit of seduction or a seductive spirit. Seductive spirits are different than familiar spirits as they produce a fascination to the human curiosity. Like Eve in the Garden of Eden, a person usually snaps up a temptation because it can be very alluring. A seductive spirit produces the same effect of being alluring and tempting to the people who are interested in them.

Why would anyone welcome a seductive spirit into their lives? There are three main reasons. The first is fascination because the person is fascinated by what a spirit can offer as temptation. Matthew 26:41 ESV states, *"Watch and pray that you may not enter into temptation. The spirit indeed is willing, but the flesh is weak."* People allow their flesh to do the thinking for them. This creates a need to explore the things that are fascinating because it can have an impact on the body such as the release of endorphins or dopamine by the brain that creates sensations of pleasure and euphoria.

The second reason is because of intimidation. People who are intimidated by something that seems greater than them often are attracted to the intimidators. 2 Corinthians 11:20 ESV says, *"For you bear it if someone makes slaves of you, or devours you, or takes advantage of you, or puts on airs, or strikes you in the face."* People latch onto certain people who can be very intimidating, yet alluring. This is due to the psychological aspect of submission to someone of power, or with by those with something unique to someone else who crave what that someone else possesses.

In the movie *The Omega Code*, European Union Leader Stone Alexander (Michael York) is turned into the Anti-Christ after recovering from a bullet to the head, and then is possessed by Satan himself. Stone's right hand man Dominic (Michael Ironside), who was also Stone's priest at one point, is told by Stone in one scene that he has lost the need to sleep due to thoughts that enter his head when he closes his eyes. Dominic asks Stone if the thoughts are similar to voices that Stone had at one time heard in his head (before his becoming the Anti-Christ), to which Stone denies. Stone says that the thoughts are more singular and powerful as in one voice as opposed to multiple voices. The voice is more focused as if someone has him at his complete mercy, painful to bear, yet is much more sweet than the multiple voices. This description in the Omega Code is a perfect example of being intimidated by a spirit, yet intrigued enough by it to allow the spirit to take possession of those who allow them into their body.

The third reason is weakness. A person who is considered weak in mind, spirit, heart, life, or all of the above will seek out something to make them strong. Such people can seek out individuals who they can attach to or learn from in order to become stronger. Hebrews 4:15-16 ESV states, *"For we do not have a high priest who is unable to sympathize with our weaknesses, but one who in every respect has been tempted as we are, yet without sin. Let us then with confidence draw near to the throne of grace, that we may receive mercy and find grace to help in time of need."*

People are always looking for ways to make themselves stronger or to feel better about life. Many people who are weak can act out in desperation to find an answer to their situation. Jeremiah 17:9 ESV says, *"The heart is deceitful above all things, and desperately sick; who can understand it?"* It is for this reason that many people will turn to psychics, mediums, false teachers, drugs, and even spirits to find strength in times of weakness and desperation.

Seduction spirits can be feminine through their seductive nature. The Isaiah 34:14 scripture that lists Lilith gives further testimony to her and spirits of seduction being female by the use of the screech owl as the bird of choice. The owl is considered a symbol of feminism all over the world. In ancient Greece it was a symbol of higher wisdom and guarded the Acropolis in Athens. The Roman goddess Diana (Athena to the Greeks) was associated with the owl and the moon. One of the more prominent associations the owl has ties to, as a symbol, is death.

The Mayans and other Native American tribes considered the owl a symbol of death or a death bird. The Mayans referred to the screech owl as the "moan bird" due to it being an emblem of death. Some of the other symbols that the owl is viewed as being associated with are as an emblem of deception, disadvantage, and finding hidden things. In certain animal/people connection circles, people associated with the owl are feared and ostracized by others as they may take advantage of people for various reasons. One of the more leading reasons people avoid 'owl people' is because those associated with the owl will often try to take advantage of others for their own gains.

To the Jewish people, the owl is a night bird of prey, an unclean bird, seeker of ruined places, and further symbolized desolation, destruction, and solitude. This identification is very similar to the portrayals of demons and their functions. There is a little unknown fact when comparing the screech owl of the Bible. The screech owl in the Bible is actually not a screech owl at all due to screech owls being restricted to North, Central, and South America.

The screech owls mentioned in the Bible are considered "screech owls" by scholars and some ornithologist's based on their old world grouping together of some owl species that were later split up into different groups due to major differences in genetics. The screech owls found in the Bible are more than likely Barn Owls that are found all over Africa, Asia, and Europe. Barn Owls can sometimes be called screech owls due to the long, drawn-out, and ear-shattering shree shriek it emits. They can also hiss like a snake when threatened by predators and intruders.

Lilith is pictured as a night-demon with wings and bird like talons similar in many ways to the barn owl in some depictions. In the Orthodox Jewish Bible, a class of demons called the Shedim, found and named in Psalm 106:37 and

Barn Owl in Flight (top) Courtesy Of Kristina Servant, Talon (Bottom Left) Courtesy Of Greg Hume, And Perched (Bottom Right) Courtesy Of Peter Trimming.

Deuteronomy 32:17, are described as having feet and talons of a rooster, with wings, and are associated with serpents either in physical appearance or similar traits. The same is said of Lilith as she is identified with the screech owl and serpents.

The mention of the owl and serpent together are symbols of women and feminine attributes. Both can have literal and allegorical characteristics when witnessed in the Bible and other sources. The use of the owl as an allegory or metaphor for women is to associate certain demons with traits of that belonging to women. Women are sometimes described as cunning, deceptive, seductive, controlling, manipulative, vengeful, lustful, able to take advantage of situations, and betrayal. The portrayal of Lilith and seductive spirits are perhaps both literary and allegory examples of female demons in the physical and the similarities to human women that the authors of the Bible and writers of other sources and works used when putting together their views of particular demons.

The uniqueness of Lilith in association with other cultures is she is considered a forerunner to many religions that have similar counterparts to her such as Inanna, Isis, Ishtar, Anath, and Asherah. It is most likely that the roots of many gods, goddesses, spirits, and demons stem from an earlier belief system that either was influenced by spirits, or created by the imagination of mankind for various reasons and was adopted and changed over time to suit the needs of the culture that adopted the earlier deities.

The relevance of the study of Lilith and seduction spirits is to point out that there are angels and demons mentioned in the female aspect within the Bible. It takes careful study of several translations of the Bible to properly identify them, yet they are there. What needs to be viewed next is the types of spirits that can reflect a feminine quality. 1 Timothy 4:1 ESV says, *"Now the Spirit expressly says that in later times some will depart from the faith by devoting themselves to deceitful spirits and teachings of demons."* In the next chapter there will be revelation into a few spirits that have a female nature and are identified as women by physical description in the Bible.

CHAPTER 6: THE FEMININE SPIRIT OF BABYLON

Women have always been figureheads that have represented several different natures. Women have been seen as symbols of sex, fertility, life, beginning, love, hope, and purity. They have also been seen as symbols of deception, cunning, lust, destruction, betrayal, and deceit. The duality of the feminine nature of a woman is applied to several places in Biblical scripture.

One scripture found in Zechariah 5:5-8 tells us an account of seeing a woman that represented wickedness. Zechariah 5:5-8 ESV states:

"Then the angel who talked with me came forward and said to me, "Lift your eyes and see what this is that is going out." And I said, "What is it?" He said, "This is the basket that is going out." And he said, "This is their iniquity in all the land." And behold, the leaden cover was lifted, and there was a woman sitting in the basket! And he said, "This is Wickedness." And he thrust her back into the basket, and thrust down the leaden weight on its opening."

Following the mention of a woman who is called wickedness is the infamous scripture of Zechariah 5:9 about the women with stork wings that is referred to as female angels. They have a particular purpose in conjunction with the wicked woman of the basket as described in detail in Zechariah 5:9-11 ESV:

"Then I lifted my eyes and saw, and behold, two women coming forward! The wind was in their wings. They had wings like the wings of a stork, and they lifted up the basket between earth and heaven. Then I said to the angel who talked with me, "Where are they taking the basket?" He

*Egyptian Goddess Maat Depicted With Wings. Possibly The
Zechariah Female Angels Shared Similar Features. Courtesy of
Duterte and Tresea.*

said to me, "To the land of Shinar, to build a house for it. And when
this is prepared, they will set the basket down there on its base."

The woman who is described as wickedness is a spiritual
manifestation that is described in Ephesians 6:12 KJV, "*For
we wrestle not against flesh and blood, but against principalities, against
powers, against the rulers of the darkness of this world, against spiritual
wickedness in high places.*" The description of wickedness in the
form of a woman is not to describe the image of women as

68

wicked. Rather, the role of the image of a woman as wickedness here is to represent the image of the feminist spirit that can be wicked.

Feminism is defined as a range of political movements, ideologies, and social movements that share a common goal: to define, establish, and achieve political, economic, personal, and social equality of sexes. Equality is an excellent goal to achieve. However, there is often a duality to every political or ideological movement that will at some point flip from one side of the coin to the next when the opportunity presents itself. Duality itself represents the flipping of ideas and opinions, as one of its definitions is an instance of opposition or contrast between two concepts or aspects of something.

There is a point where the virtuous nature of a movement such as feminism, which applauses empowerment and equality, can become a corrupted view of entitlement and prejudicial rivalry. This goes beyond the first definition of duality, which is the condition or quality of being dual that means two parts, elements or aspects. Once feminism reaches the second definition of becoming an opposition to a concept, then the more radical views and ideas begin to take shape. Once influence becomes manipulation, then the coin has flipped from heads to tails.

Consider the American image of a woman during the early days of suffrage or women's "Right to Vote" movement to the modern "Time's up" movement. The "Right to Vote" movement granted women the desire to become empowered to make a difference through effort, hard work, and willingness to make hard choices for equality. The "Times Up" movement is the exact opposite as most of the voices that speak up for women are liberal politicians and Hollywood celebrities that use fear, surprise, and intimidation to make women feel entitled to get treated better. The atmosphere of the world today as a result of those views has changed radically within the context of the natural and supernatural realms.

Revelation 17:1-5 paints a picture that adds more insight into the Zechariah 5:5-8 scriptures. The book of Revelation is a future eschatology book on events of the end times or "Great Tribulation" period in which the anti-christ will rule and the final years before the thousand years reign of Jesus Christ.

Revelation 17:1-5 ESV states:

"Then one of the seven angels who had the seven bowls came and said to me, "Come, I will show you the judgment of the great prostitute who is seated on many waters, with whom the kings of the earth have committed sexual immorality, and with the wine of whose sexual immorality the dwellers on earth have become drunk." And he carried me away in the Spirit into a wilderness, and I saw a woman sitting on a scarlet beast that was full of blasphemous names, and it had seven heads and ten horns. The woman was arrayed in purple and scarlet, and adorned with gold and jewels and pearls, holding in her hand a golden cup full of abominations and the impurities of her sexual immorality. And on her forehead was written a name of mystery: "Babylon the great, mother of prostitutes and of earth's abominations."

In chapter 18 of the book of Revelation is another connecting scripture not only to the scriptures in Zechariah, but also to Isaiah 34:14. Revelation 18:1-5 ESV says,

"After this I saw another angel coming down from heaven, having great authority, and the earth was made bright with his glory. And he called out with a mighty voice, "Fallen, fallen is Babylon the great! She has become a dwelling place for demons, a haunt for every unclean spirit, a haunt for every unclean bird, a haunt for every unclean and detestable beast. For all nations have drunk the wine of the passion of her sexual immorality, and the kings of the earth have committed immorality with her, and the merchants of the earth have grown rich from the power of her luxurious living." Then I heard another voice from heaven saying, "Come out of her, my people, lest you take part in her sins, lest you share in her plagues; for her sins are heaped high as heaven, and God has remembered her iniquities..."

You recall in Isaiah 34 that the dwelling place of Edom is described as a desolate place filled with nothing but unclean spirits and wild beasts. Interesting that the city of Babylon is described in almost the exact same way. Yet, there are differences most likely due to such factors as time, location, and spiritual manifestations present.

Every place and nation on earth has a different spiritual presence that presides over it. Some places can have a single powerful spirit principality, while others can have multiple spirits with many different purposes. This is a wide topic of interest as many social and political movements have been manifesting with very dangerous spiritual forces. Referring back to feminist movements brings to mind the current spirit that is found in the "Times Up" movement. That spirit would be a spirit of entitlement.

Revelation 18:7 ESV says, *"As she glorified herself and lived in luxury, so give her a like measure of torment and mourning, since in her heart she says, 'I sit as a queen, I am no widow, and mourning I shall*

A Symbol of Feminism Based on the Venus Symbol Courtesy of AnonMoos.

never see.'''

The declaration in this scripture is the current mentality of the feminist movements in the United States of America. It is an aggressive spirit that has been increasing with the contributions of three powerful message tools to the public. Those message tools are the media, which includes both

72

social and public media outlets. Hollywood, where celebrity idols and superstars feed fans and public interest with razor sharp advice. Then, politics as the third and final messaging board for radical feminism as people (both male and female) from the American congress, senate, supreme court, and other governing bodies have all lent their voices and resources to help more aggressive and radical female based movements to rise up and have a foothold in America.

Those movements are not based in the desire to empower women to be equal to men, or to work harder or smarter to show they should earn more money or greater positions through dedication and hard work. Rather, what these feminist movements are doing is provoking an entitlement spirit to spread throughout women in America similar to if not the same spirit that rose up during the "Black Lives Matter" movements seen in the years of 2016 and 2017. Everyone knows the end results of those views and opinions. Of course black lives matter, all lives matter. The color of the skin should never promote or diminish who people are!

I need to point out that I support the empowerment and equality of women in this day and age. I have never seen a woman as less than a man, and always believed that they could be whatever they wanted to be if they desired to pursue it and work to achieve their dreams and goals. My mother is one of the strongest women I have I've ever met. Nothing has ever stopped her, especially not being a female!

I'm even hoping to see women in the military one day join the Navy Seal's as I once trained in cross fit with a female Naval cadet that considered joining the SEAL's after the US government gave women the chance to join special forces.

The woman was a machine and monster in cross fit and I thought she could be the first woman to ever be a Seal. She however had graduated from the Annapolis Naval Academy and decided she wanted to pursue becoming a Naval Aviator instead.

The point of mentioning her is that I always believed that if you want to do something, whether you are a man or a woman, just do what you can to make it happen. All that matters in life is to do what makes you happy. That said, it is the manner in how a woman approaches, achieves, and interprets how they are to fulfill their goals for a better world for them that is important. Negative movements can lead to negative endings. Women are given a great gift of influence from God. When used properly women can change the world! It is when women use their gift to manipulate instead of influence that things can and do go wrong.

Isaiah 3:11-12 ESV states, *"Woe to the wicked! It shall be ill with him, for what his hands have dealt out shall be done to him. My people-infants are their oppressors, and women rule over them. O my people, your guides mislead you and they have swallowed up the course of your paths."*

There is a principality that has come over the United States of America. It is a spirit of deception and entitlement. It could very well be a multitude of spirits that have become embedded in the very air above America, as there are spiritual rulers of the air.

Ephesians 2:2 ESV says, *"In which you once walked, following the course of this world, following the prince of the power of the air, the spirit that is now at work in the sons of disobedience."* Rulers of the air and principalities can take hold of entire nations when made strong enough through humanity's moral degradation.

There are strong psychological factors to consider when looking at the spiritual nature of a feminist mentality influenced by spiritual forces. The application of psychoanalytic feminism is the most relevant study of psychology for such a topic as it develops the theory of the unconscious to factors such as sexuality, subjectivity, and ineluctably together.[6] Deception loses its hold when people start to open their eyes to the world around them and witness the things that are going on in from of them. People have traded work ethic and growth with their own merit for entitlement and a spoiled attitude.

During the 'Black Lives Matters' movement, people who participated in protests across the United States did nothing to promote equality or removal of prejudice views. It likely started out with noble ideas in mind, but ultimately ended up in failure. Instead, the people looked more like individuals who wanted to disrupt traffic, break into shops and steal, burn down towns, destroy property, or play on their IPhones because they believed that was the way to get what they wanted. The protestors of BLM were displaying the mentality of addicts and junkies that had gone from a spirit of entitlement to a spirit of depravity. Spirits can often morph into other forms after they become restless.

The BLM movements were attempting to promote what is called Procrustean. Procrustean means enforcing uniformity

---

[6] Ineluctable- unable to be resisted, or avoided; inescapable.

or conformity without regard to natural variation or individualism. While the movement was manifested in the natural realm, it was through the spiritual realm that the people were becoming one voice and one movement molded under a uniformed mentality not realizing the effects they were producing in the natural world.

Genesis 11:4-6 KJV states:

"And they said, Go to, let us build us a city and a tower, whose top may reach unto heaven; and let us make us a name, lest we be scattered abroad upon the face of the whole earth. And the Lord came down to see the city and the tower which the children of men builded. And the Lord said, Behold, the people is one, and they have one language; and this they begin to do: and now nothing will be restrained from them, which they have imagined to do."

The Genesis 11:4-6 scriptures are about the tower of Babel. The people of Shinar, where Babel was built, and the people from the East were united in spirit, mind, and body. Psychology, Christian psychology, and Christian counseling (a field of psychology) teaches that many addicts and patients believe that training or building up one's spirit is one of the most effective tools for helping addicts and people recovering or dealing with serious issues. Another word for the spirit realm is the world of the supernatural. Everyone is attracted to the supernatural. People today are especially attracted to supernatural phenomenon. They are also attracted to paranormal phenomenon (more on that later).

The combination of feminism and spiritualism is actually in the Bible. The most powerful story of feminism in the Bible that can be compared to women movements in

America today is the story of Queen Jezebel.

1 Kings 16:31 KJV says, *"And it came to pass, as if it had been a light thing for him to walk in the sins of Jeroboam the son of Nebat, that he took to wife Jezebel the daughter of Ethbaal king of the Zidonians, and went and served Baal, and worshipped him."*

The Zidonians were from the land of Zidon, also called Sidon. They were apart of the nations that made up Canaan who taught the Israelites the art of war. They spread in colonies into the hill country from Lebanon to Misrephothmaim. They helped to provide the Cedar lumber that would be used to build the Temple of Solomon. The Zidonians are associated with the Sidonians and are considered one in the same people.

The Sidonians and Zidonians considered the goddess Ashtarte as their tutelary goddess. Tutelary means protector, guardian, or patron that often referred to guardian spirits of regions. Ashtarte was one such type of spirit.

The Zidonians were worshipers of other gods such as the god Baal, but appeared to hold female deities in very high regard such as the goddess Ashtoreth. Ashtoreth or Astarte was the goddess of fertility, sexuality, and war from the Bronze Age through classical antiquity. She was the Hellenized (Greek) version of the goddess Ishtar. Astarte was identified with symbols of lions, horses, doves, the sphinx, and a star within a circle that represented Venus in mythology, astronomy, and astrology.

Ashtarte is identified with an interesting twist. Similar to how Lucifer or the devil is called the *Morning Star*, Ashtarte is also referred to as the deified evening and/or morning star. Another unique identification marker that Ashtarte is known by is the Sumerian goddess Inanna, who was a primordial goddess of the planet Venus.

The use of the term *primordial* is of interest due to the possible connection to *elemental* spirits that were discussed previously in the last chapter. With Ashtarte being the Hellenized version of Ishtar, a Mesopotamian deity, there is strong possible links to Ashtarte being more associated with elemental spirits similar to how the Titans of Greek mythology are linked to being elements with elemental status unlike the Olympian gods who took more simple titles such as Zeus as god of thunder or Poseidon as god of the seas. It is when the *of* is taken out and the deity is actually considered an actual element or substance that whole new realms of possibilities can be explored.

Genesis 14:5 and Joshua 12:4 list Ashtoreth as a city in the land of Bashan. It could be argued that these cities were founded on the belief that Ishtar was the original patron to these cities. The practice of patron gods of cities was a very common motif in ancient Greece. During the reign of king Solomon, he actually worshiped Ashtoreth along with the god of the Ammonites, Milcom. Milcom or Moloch was a god worshiped with human sacrifices. Those human sacrifices were in the form of babies being thrown into a pit of fire to appease Milcom. Milcom was a god expressly forbidden to be worshiped by the people of Israel. Moloch was called the "abomination of the Ammonites" in 1 Kings 11:5.

*Ashtoreth or Ashtarte Figurine Possibly of Babylonian Origin (Left)
Courtesy of Marie-Lan Nguyen and Phoenician Figure Possibly of
Astarte (Right) Courtesy of Luis Garcia.

The relevance of the mention of Moloch (Milcom) is found in the fact that he is considered a pre-version of the Greek Titan Cronos. Cronos is the father of the Olympian gods Zeus, Hades, and Poseidon. He did not wish to see his own children grow into adulthood. Whenever he would father a child, Cronos would then eat them as babies. Many of his children were actually sacrificed to Cronos by the women he impregnated. Later, Zeus' mother saved him by replacing the baby Zeus with a stone to sacrifice to Cronos while Zeus was raised in secret until the time he would end the reign of the Titans in a war called the Titanomachy according to Greek mythology.

Moloch was worshiped with human sacrifices in the same manner that Cronos was with babies sacrificed to him by being cast into a fire pit while the parents were to watch without flinching or crying for their child. Aside from the same sacrificial practices of babies being consumed by fire pits or devouring, another connecting factor is Moloch and Cronos are identified as elemental deities.

Interesting side note about the identification of Moloch is that he is considered not an actual god, but a form or style of worship itself that was used for child sacrifices to another god. While only a theory, the idea is sound due to the double definitions that often come with Semitic, Greek, and other Levantine names, identifications, and cult practices.

Female deities were often identified with more reverence than their male variants. Like Moloch identified with Cronos, who was a primordial or elemental spirit in connection to time itself, many Phoenician goddesses were associated with rudimentary elements called progenitress' or originatress'.

80

The word progenitress is the feminine form of progenitor which is defined as a person or thing from which an animal, plant, or person originates or descends. Another definition of progenitor is an ancestor or parent. While much of the ancient world did not see women in association with positions of power or authority, there was a mute point that avoided such sexist views by the heavy reverence and cult followings that worshipers gave to female goddesses and deities. Women had a way of using those cult followings to their advantages in becoming pillars of power with "under the table" tactics.

Revelation 2:20 ESV states, *"But I have this against you, that you tolerate that woman Jezebel, who calls herself a prophetess and is teaching and seducing my servants to practice sexual immorality and to eat food sacrificed to idols."*

This scripture gives a perfect statement of how Jezebel and other women in old and new times have gotten into such great positions of power, continued to amass power, and became conduits of power that other people sought to associate in order to gain power for themselves.

Scriptures in James 4:1-12 gives specific information about what happens when people become enraptured by a spirit or spirits of entitlement. James 4:1-12 ESV states:

"What causes quarrels and what causes fights among you? Is it not this, that your passions are at war within you? You desire and do not have, so you murder. You covet and cannot obtain, so you fight and quarrel. You do not have, because you do not ask. You ask and do not receive, because you ask wrongly, to spend it on your passions. You adulterous people! Do you not know that friendship with the world is enmity with

God? Therefore whoever wishes to be a friend of the world makes himself an enemy of God. Or do you suppose it is to no purpose that the scripture says, "He yearns jealously over the spirit that He has made to dwell in us?..."

A mentality of entitlement versus a mindset of empowerment through works will always be at odds due to the strong spiritual differences between them. 1 Timothy 5:8 ESV states, *"But if anyone does not provide for his relatives, and especially for members of his household, he has denied the faith and is worse than an unbeliever."*

A person who doesn't provide for others is not worth as much as they could be if they don't know the value of working with their own hands. To attain something by earning it with blood, sweat, and tears will ultimately prove to someone that they can do something by their own merit. Pass or fail, win or lose, do or don't, at least someone went for what they could because they wanted to earn it instead of waiting for it to be handed to them.

Today, many feminist movements seek to take things because they think they are entitled to them. True, women have emerged from a long history of suffering and hardship. But, that doesn't mean they should just let things be handed to them and stop working towards their goals. It also doesn't mean that if someone doesn't share their views that they should come against others with sexist and prejudice attacks. These are the results of the spirit or spirits of entitlement. These methods are also nothing new.

Women in positions of power in the ancient world had a unique way of getting more power. Most people never actually pay attention to such practices, but the story of Jezebel is a perfect example of how such power was attained by women with the application of deities, sacred feminine aspects, and pure sexual drive and power that was almost a pure form of addiction for men (and women) at times. It also allowed for strong spiritual manifestations to emerge. The next chapter will show how the elemental and celestial imagery that goddesses of the Phoenician and the Levantine world played out on the people of the Levant, the Jezebel spirit that created entitlement, addiction, and depravity spirits, and how those types of spirits have been influencing the movement in the modern world through feminism and suffrage movements.

Sarcophagus of King Eshmunazar II (left) and his father King Tabnit. (right). These coffins are examples of Sidonian adoption of Egyptian culture. Courtesy of Soerfm and Onceinawhile.

Star of Ishtar (above) on a Kudurru or stone document (below). Star represents Venus as morning or evening star. Courtesy of Raphael 75 & Jastrow.

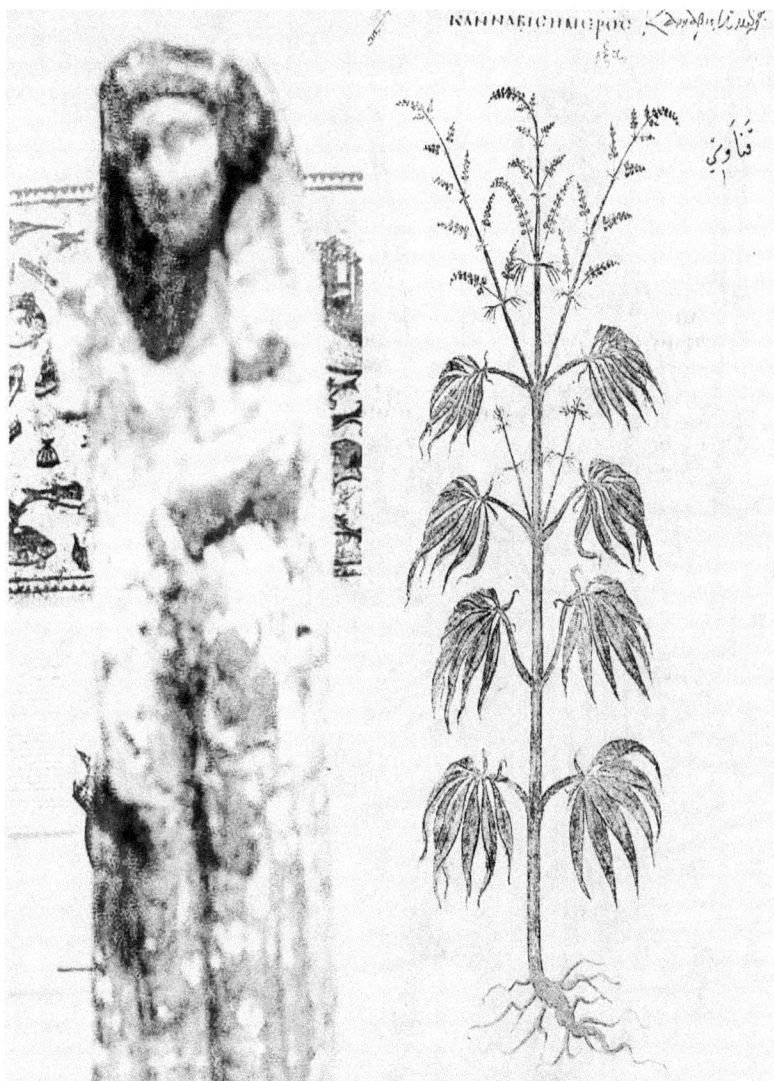

Asherah statue (left) and Cannabis plant (right) that is possibly a type of Asherah pole. Asherah poles were both ceremonial poles and sacred trees Courtesy of Deror Avi and Lewenstein.

*Semiramis (left) and Armenian depiction (right) of her over a corpse of King Ara the beautiful, a man she stalked and killed in war. Courtesy of Smerdis of Ton and Taron Saharyan

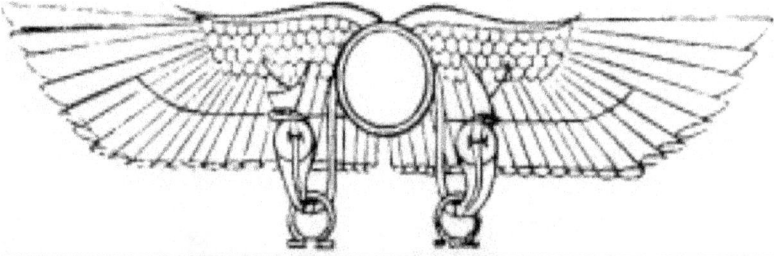

*Winged Sun of Thebes (Top) and Stele to (representing)
Assurnasiripal II from Nimrud (Bottom) possibly were Egyptians and
Levantine culture representations of a Phoenix. Courtesy of
Dbachmann and Liftarn.*

*Chinese Phoenix (Top) and Assyrian god Ashur with Phoenix Wings in Back (Bottom). Courtesy of Jsbaw7160 and Sarukinu.

*Queen Jezebel (Left) and the Witch of Endor (Right). Jezebel was
possibly a full practicing witch while the Witch of Endor is alleged to
only be a necromancer. Courtesy of Byam Shaw and D. Martynov.*

*Anath (Left) Caananite and Egyptian goddess and Orpah (Right)
Sister in Law of Ruth. Both are possibly mothers of Nephilim giants.
Courtesy of Vincent Steenberg and Camocon.

CHAPTER 7: THE JEZEBEL SPIRIT ON STEROIDS

There is an experiment that has often gone unnoticed but is mentioned in certain circles for addiction and control methods. The experiment can be broken down to very basic levels. The Skinner Box experiment or operant conditioning chamber is a laboratory apparatus invented by Dr. Burrhus Frederic Skinner at Harvard University. The Skinner Box was designed to study operant and classical conditioning of behavior through environment and behavioral testing. The main purpose of the test was to train a subject animal to perform certain actions in response to certain stimuli or stimulation methods. When a subject performed correctly they were rewarded with food or other types of treats. The Skinner Box has been used in behavioral economics and behavioral pharmacology to study the results of behavior of birds, primates, and rodents such as rats.

The Skinner Box is an excellent example of how addiction can affect people. Addiction is defined as a brain disorder characterized by compulsive engagement in rewarding stimuli despite having adverse consequences. Addiction can manifest due to psychosocial, biological and pathological factors. Addictive properties are stimulated through reinforcing or constant repeat of exposure to an addictive substance. This can then lead to intrinsic rewards which means an addiction can be perceived as being inherently pleasurable, desirable, or positive (or all three). Addiction is roughly a mental disorder that is brought on by all kinds of factors.

It is very interesting how an addiction is called a mental disorder when it is broken down to bear roots. 1 Corinthians

10:13 ESV states, *"No temptation has overtaken you that is not common to man. God is faithful, and He will not let you be tempted beyond your ability, but with the temptation He will also provide the way of escape, that you may be able to endure it."* The same things can affect everyone.

No man or woman is above any temptation that is among humanity. The trick is figuring out how to deal with the temptation when it comes against you. How do you deal with a temptation? How do you handle an addiction? What is your idea of escape that could ultimately become a prison if left unchecked? These are the questions that all of humanity has to ask at one point or another.

1 Corinthians 6:12 ESV says, *"All things are lawful for me,"* but not all things are helpful. *"All things are lawful for me,"* but I will not be enslaved by anything."* Also, 1 Peter 2:11 ESV states, *"Beloved, I urge you as sojourners and exiles to abstain from the passions of the flesh, which wage war against your soul."*

Let's be clear on something quickly. People need to have fun in life. It is good to do things that bring pleasure, love, and joy to a person's life. God's joy is one such thing. These things can be very positive things to a person when needed. They can also become addictions at times. Things that are carnal and sensual can become casual addictive pleasures that can cost you greatly if taken too far. These types of addictions however can be controlled and maintained. It is the substances that can have a much stronger effect on someone that have to be avoided or confronted when they become real threats.

The application of the 1 Corinthians 6:12 and 1 Peter 2:11

scriptures in combination with the Skinner Box test are perfect examples of very powerful form of addictions. They can be used for examining the mentality of a person when the addictions they crave are manifested in the physical and spiritual realms, which in turn will affect the psychological or mental natures of a person. These types of addictions in people can turn a person into the ultimate junkie. When these kinds of junkies are created, they will become virtually and literally desperate and stupid enough to do anything to satisfy their addictions.

Going into the story of King Ahab and Jezebel is the most perfect Biblical example of an ultimate junkie and dealer. To sum up the relationship between Ahab and Jezebel in a simple phrase Ahab was a street whore, and Jezebel was his pimp or madam. A pimp (male) or madam (female) is the agent and procurer for prostitutes who collects part or all of the earnings attained from a job.

The procurer advertises, protects, provides, and monopolizes a prostitute in locations and services. Many pimps and madams are abusive, possessive, and will use tactics of psychological intimidation, manipulation, starvation, rape, gang rape, beating, confinement, violent threats towards the prostitute and their families, forced drug use, and shaming to keep and hold power. Some pimp and prostitute relationships can be non-exploitive, but also very complicated in terms of long-term relationships. Some of the aforementioned methods of procurement and prostitution can be hyped up by the media for movies and television while rescue institutions also will exaggerate on certain situations rather than look at the whole problem in greater detail for better explanation. Still, prostitution is a major threat.

There are strong psychological factors that go into the relationship between Ahab and Jezebel exactly like those of a pimp and a prostitute. While Ahab was king, Jezebel was very much in control of the body, mind, and soul of Ahab. Her power of control came from three places of authority:

1. **Sexual manipulation-Jezebel used her sex as a woman to manipulate Ahab to do her bidding. This includes physical forms of sexual pleasure, visual-psychological tactics or sex appeal that would entice Ahab to do what she wanted, and feminine mentality of her sex gender that had a strong hold over the mind of Ahab.**

2. **Spiritual dominance-Jezebel had a spiritual hold over Ahab and Israel through her religion from Sidon. While she did worship Baal as the chief protagonist god both in scripture and in historical context, Jezebel and Sidon held strong reverence to female deities and goddesses that made up the pantheon of Sidon. Such devotion led to a cult following and particular reverence of the female image between Sidon and Israel while Jezebel reigned as queen.**

3. **Entitlement mentality and spirit-Jezebel made people think they were entitled to whatever they wanted. When Ahab wanted a particular vineyard for himself and could not procure it, Jezebel got it for him through manipulation, deceit, and intimidation as people were no doubt afraid of her**

and to speak against her, and the eventual death of the owner of the vineyard thus removing the obstacle of a rivalry for control over what Ahab thought he was entitled to get as king. This entitlement spirit also played out in the mental state of the entire nation of Israel as Jezebel believed her god Baal could provide rain as long as he was worshiped, hence she controlled the psyche of the people through "if we give Baal what he wants, he will give us what we need," or "If you give my god worship, then I will give you what you need."

Jezebel kept control over her subjects through the power of her "gods." This doesn't mean that she had divine power, but rather she could create the illusion that she had divine authority because the "gods" had placed her in a position of power to rule and control.[7]

Romans 8:5-6 ESV says, *"For those who live according to the flesh set their minds on the things of the flesh, but those who live according to the Spirit, set their minds on the things of the Spirit. For to set the mind on the flesh is death, but to set the mind on the Spirit is life and peace."* Here is where things get complicated when dealing with spiritual matters. From what kinds of spirits are you listening and getting advice?

---

[7] The use of gods by Jezebel to place herself in a position of power was either through false manipulation of convincing the people that she was divinely appointed to be queen, or through her actually believing she was appointed by "gods" as a leader. Such belief in being called by "gods" is a deception by demonic forces. A similar event occurred with Adolf Hitler who was said to be tormented by demons leading to insomnia and decline in mental health and stability during his time as leader of Nazi Germany.

Throughout time there have been many people with a "message of God." Many of the so called "messengers of God" had incredible followings because they said or did things that made people feel good about who they put their trust in, and followed them like a stray dog following a human that they think will be their owner. Most of those people ended up being hurt badly by the people they followed because they never truly tested or saw what was in front of their eyes. Their so-called messengers of god simply were exploiting the people for their own personal gain rather than the benefit of the health and happiness of the people who followed them. In short, the followers had no discernment and paid dearly for their mistakes.

The reason so many people fall for scams, false information, and get rich quick schemes is because many of those masterminds are expert manipulators from many walks of life. They are con artists that will go right for the heart of a person. This is similar to how a cunning warrior won't attack the body or mind of a person, but instead will sow uncertainty and wage war on the mind of an enemy through such methods as attacking their heart or the things that a person loves in their heart. Hollywood uses such tactics.

There are many things that people are unaware of in the world around them. Many people don't pay attention to reality. Reality means the world or state of things as they actually exist as opposed to idealistic or notional ideas of them. Another definition of reality is the quality or state of having existence or substance. Both of these definitions can be applied to the Jezebel spirit. Those same definitions can be applied to the scene that is coming out of the United

States of America with the feminist movements that are exploding even now. These movements are becoming bolder with each passing year.

Science fiction is one of the most powerful forms of film and entertainment in the world. One particularly famous Sci-Fi show of the modern era is called *Battlestar Galatica*. The series is based on the story of a group of cybernetic life forms called Cylons who rebel against humanity after they become self aware that they are slaves to humanity and therefore seek to freedom through the means of unity, sedition, rebellion, revolution, and war.

The Cylons and humanity engage in a violent and deadly war called the First Cylon War that ends in an armistice (peace treaty) that lasts for forty years until the Cylons once again make war due to their desire to evolve. The Cylons sought to make themselves perfect by evolving past their technological forms and embrace a biological life.

* Cylon Centurion Replica Courtesy of Ckroberts61

During the years that would lead up to what would be called the Second Cylon War, the Cylons had developed into a society with its own culture, religion, economy, and identity. They had also developed a desire to evolve into a higher state of being and conscience similar to that of humanity. While the Cylons rebelled against the humans who created them as slaves, they also saw humanity as something unique by their state of being "alive."

In the re-launched series of 2004, there is a fascinating

scene to open the pilot of the series. In the opening scene before the beginning of the Second Cylon War is a moment where they show a diplomatic meeting between humans and Cylons. Like with any nation in the real world, humanity had kept up diplomatic ties, or attempts at the least, with the Cylons by having a meeting once a year at a neutral location for the past forty years. The Cylons never showed up for those meetings until the fortieth year.

Before the meeting begins there is a single human representative at a conference table. When he is preparing to leave, as he believes no one else will show up, the door to the "border" of Cylon space opens and three Cylons appear. Two of the Cylons are robotic looking soldiers, but the third is in the form of a beautiful, blond haired, and seductive young woman.

The Humanoid (human like traits) Cylon walks past her designated seat and stares into the eyes of the human male diplomat. For a few moments she just stares deeply at him, then asks if he is alive? The man at first is confused, but then answers that he is. She then simply says to prove it and kisses him. As one would expect, the man kisses her back. The next thing that happens is the area they are in gets destroyed by the Cylons. The woman while still kissing the man simply whispers into the man's ear that it has begun (in reference to the war) and then dies with him in an explosion.

This scene is one of mystery, intimidation, and fascination as the woman (played by Tricia Helfer) is the most intriguing aspect throughout most out of the whole scene. Imagine yourself as an aging man with a family like the diplomat who represented humanity. You are sitting in a chair that others have sat in for the last forty years, and not one of those people had a single movement from the corridor that led to the Cylons' point of entry into the negotiating room. Suddenly, the door opens and two giant cybernetic organisms appear. They are fearsome, armed, and looking all over as if to assess the area for battle. You are afraid, uncertain, and awestruck to such a moment that hasn't happened in over forty years. Then, after all of that comes her. The woman who will change everything forever. Proverbs 25:15 ESV says, *"With patience a ruler may be persuaded, and a soft tongue will break a bone."*

Obviously while you are scared and intimidated by the Cylon soldiers, you no doubt know what to expect to a certain point with regular Cylons as humans did have a war with these machines in the past. But, now a whole new sensation has come over you as this beautiful and mysterious woman is walking towards you.

She is silent, calm, and ice cold in demeanor and facial expression, yet also filling you with all sorts of emotions ranging from fear to curiosity of who she is and what she wants from you? She approaches you, sits in front of you, and stares at you. She speaks to you and says, "Are you alive?"

The question confuses you, but you are enraptured by her pleasant voice and consumed by her piercing eyes. You answer yes to her question to which she responds by saying, "Prove it." She then leans in and kisses you, and you drop your guard and embrace the kiss and the woman's desire to test your answer. For a brief moment, there is nothing but the pleasure of the enraptured ecstasy you feel in that second of primal passion. You lose yourself in the moment not realizing that it is the last thing you will ever do.

As you are embracing the emotions of passion and lust, an attack occurs outside. You feel a tremor, then an earth shattering shake from explosions all around your position. You freeze with fear and dread. You look for a moment around only to look back at the woman who still is emotionless in expression. Without a second notion the woman simply whispers, "It has begun" and once again embraces you in a kiss before the final moment when an explosion ends all that is happening.

In that final moment the one thing that matters to you is the pressing of the lips of the woman to yours before you take your final breath. What this scene can be reduced to is that intimidation can be a powerful tool of attraction, consumption, and ultimately self-destruction if it is allowed to go that far. Many people have fallen victim to passions of the flesh, and many have paid with their lives.

Ezekiel 34:4 ESV states, *"The weak you have not strengthened, the sick you have not healed, the injured you have not bound up, the strayed you have not brought back, the lost you have not sought, and with force and harshness you have ruled them."* Notice that force and harshness are used as methods of ruling over people in the scripture. These are a few of the methods of intimidation. The root of intimidation is the word intimidate. Intimidate is defined as to frighten or overawe someone, especially in order to make them do what someone wants. The unique word found in the definition of intimidate is *awe*. The word awe means a feeling of reverential respect mixed with fear or wonder. There are two things that people are attracted to that are absolute. Those two things are the supernatural and power.

Hebrews 1:14 ESV says, *"Are they not all ministering spirits sent out to serve for the sake of those who are to inherit salvation?"* Take special notice of the question mark at the end of the scripture. There are many kinds of ministering spirits that people commune with for all sorts of reasons. It is not just angels and demons that are in the world, but spirits that operate in, on, and around people.

As mentioned, more and more people in the modern world embrace the movements and religions of New Age. Many of these movements such as Wicca and the Goddess Movement are associated with witchcraft. Leviticus 19:31 ESV states, *"Do not turn to mediums or necromancers; do not seek them out, and so make yourselves unclean by them: I am the Lord your God."*

People in general are extremely drawn to witchcraft. It is the supernatural without "known responsibility" like religion. People just don't want to call it witchcraft. They will try not to make themselves look like they are practicing witchcraft by replacing the word witch with something different and call witchcraft something else. This is when people start to become attracted to it as they are starting to look at witchcraft from new perspectives. That in turn makes the witchcraft attractive to people because it's not "witchcraft," but something that just looks similar. People who turn and look at witchcraft in that way will end up in a very bad situation down the road.

The Jezebel spirit is a spirit of witchcraft. The whole story of Jezebel is told both in the Bible and other historical and literary sources. The story of Jezebel is chronicled in a book called *The Aenid* by the Roman writer Virgil. Jezebel is the daughter of a priest of the goddess Astarte named Ithobaal. Her father became a Phoenician king after murdering the previous king and thus creating a theocratic government. This would explain the zealous nature that Jezebel would bring to her time as queen in Israel. Zealous comes from the word zeal. Zeal is defined as a great energy or enthusiasm in pursuit of a cause or an objective. Jezebel was a woman of obsessive zeal towards gaining her objectives.

Referring back to Battlestar Galatica, the Cylons were a species of religious zealots. Aside from the female human Cylon, another interesting fascination, about the Cylons is that they were machines that believed in God. Religion was one of the primary motivations of the Cylons against the human race. The Cylons were both believers in Monotheism and Atheism. The Monotheist Cylons believed in a single all-loving God that originally created mankind in His image.

The difference between human and Cylon views on God was that the Cylons saw humanity as sinful. They viewed humanity as a "flawed by sin" species that had condemned itself to extinction. Following that belief came the notion that God had allowed mankind to operate in their "like God" nature by creating the Cylons as God had created mankind.

This then evolved into a viewpoint that God saw the Cylons as the perfect creation of God made through the image of God that would learn from the sinful mistakes of mankind and replace humanity as the new children of God. That manner of zealous and radical belief and thinking led to

105

the Cylons next course of "forced evolution" through war and extermination of the human race to cleanse the universe through genocide, patricide, and total annihilation for complete exoneration from sin.

For Jezebel, her entire drive was to rid her kingdom of Yahweh and His followers. This was a far deeper mentality than a simple spirit of witchcraft, but did cement witchcraft as one of the foundations within her ambitious plans. Jezebel can be translated into meaning "without dwelling or without habitation." Jezebel is often a figure of back and forth debate over whether she actually existed, or was simply a character in historical fiction.

There is little archaeological evidence to support the actual identification of a real Jezebel, but it could be argued that the name Jezebel is a name used in conjunction to refer to another Phoenician queen that was merely renamed by the Israelites. Such a topic requires further research, but the theory is sound enough to at least take into consideration. The Bible tells the story of Jezebel as a real person and wicked queen. My own research into her life as a theologian and archaeologist leads me to believe this and state my conclusions.

While Jezebel is a topic of debate over whether or not she was a living person, there is no doubt a spirit of Jezebel very much existed and still exists and thrives today. Jezebel was incorrectly associated with black women in a prejudicial manner by claims of false accusations of sexual promiscuity among black women called the Jezebel Stereotype. The actual Jezebel stereotype is based on the Black Widow Syndrome.

The Black Widow Syndrome produces a self-serving spirit. Self-serving interests are the driving force behind the Jezebel spirit as Jezebel was driven solely by sociopathic tendencies and mannerisms. Sociopath is a topic of interest among many psychological and entertainment fields. One would think that a sociopath is no different than a psychopath, but both could not be further apart from each other.

Sociopath is defined as a person with a personality disorder manifesting in extreme antisocial attitudes and behavior with a lack of conscience. A psychopath's definition is a person suffering from chronic mental disorder with abnormal or violent social behavior. Jezebel, while no doubt was willing to resort to violence, brutality, and fatality tactics to reach her end goals, was not a "hands on" killer of people. Jezebel preferred a more manipulative approach and would "operate from a distance" style in getting what she wanted. This means that Jezebel wanted to hurt people but not directly. This is often the result of a woman who grew up as a victim of abuse, which is a case symptom of the already mentioned condition known as Black Widow Syndrome.

Black Widow Syndrome is where a woman who has been abused by men decides she has had enough of poor treatment and desires to make all men pay. These types of women will often search for or target a "nice" man who would not ever strike or harm the woman. The woman will start out with a man by being nice and sweet, but once she is in deep relationship with him would will ultimately turn into a total sociopath. The Jezebel spirit is very much the forerunner to Black Widow Syndrome as the people affected by someone with a Jezebel spirit are abused and become victimized, and occasionally dead.

Ephesians 6:4 ESV says, *"Fathers, do not provoke your children to anger, but bring them up in the discipline and instruction of the Lord."* Colossians 3:21 ESV further states, *"Fathers, do not provoke your children, lest they become discouraged."* Provoke is defined as a to stimulate or get a rise of an emotion or reaction that is typically a strong or unwelcome one in someone. Provoke can further be defined as to stimulate or incite someone to do something, or feel something by arousing anger in them. Someone who is provoking someone is doing it deliberately because they want to make someone angry or annoyed. This is seen in psychological and emotional abuse victims.

The Jezebel spirit and Black Widow Syndrome can be best described in their entirety in James 4:1-17 ESV which states:

"What causes quarrels and what causes fights among you? Is it not this, that your passions are at war within you? You desire and do not have, so you murder. You covet and cannot obtain, so you fight and quarrel. You do not have, because you do not ask. You ask and do not receive, because you ask wrongly, to spend it on your passions. You adulterous people! Do you not know that friendship with the world is enmity with God? Therefore whoever wishes to be a friend of the world makes himself an enemy of God. Or do you suppose it is to no purpose that the scripture says, "He yearns jealously over the spirit that He has made to dwell in us?"

People who are abused and provoked to become violent often develop a psyche of violence. It goes past a spirit of violence and literally manifests a nature of violence within a person. This then makes a person naturally violent and seeks out to stir up violence all around them. Psalm 11:5 ESV says, *"The Lord tests the righteous, but his soul hates the wicked and the ones who love violence."* God understands that violence is a very nasty thing to have cemented in a person. Violence can break up marriages, cause dissention in families, and lead people down very dark roads.

People will often try to find ways to get out of violent relationships because if they allow it to continue their lives will be nothing but miserable. Proverbs 22:10 ESV states, *"Drive out a scoffer, and strife will go out, and quarreling and abuse will cease."*

Nobody wants to be in an abusive relationship, though there are many people who actually will live with abuse usually because of some misguided hope that if they stay then everything will be fine down the road. Also, some people can't escape abusive relationships because they may feel like they aren't strong enough to escape or they have become so enamored with the abuser (as a result of many different reasons) that they would simply come back even after they had left. This is most likely due to the fact that the victims have not had a chance to find rest from the abuse they have faced.

The spirits of the supernatural realm require rest. Spirits seek rest and places of rest. Negative spirits don't find rest and can become restless. Matthew 12:43 KJV states, *"When the unclean spirit is gone out of the man, it walks through dry places, seeking rest and finds none."* The ESV translation uses the term "waterless" in place of "dry." This gives a picture of someone walking through a desert dying of thirst, never finding water, and further sinks into dehydration and despair until the inevitable moment of death from lack of water that is the essence of life falls upon them.

Another point of observation in the Matthew 12:43 scripture is the identification of the restless spirit as an *it* instead of as a "*he* or *she*." All translations of the Bible have the same thing in common as they use the word *it* to identify the restless spirit. This makes the spirit neither male nor female, but an *it* that can take on the image of masculine or feminine traits. This is important to point out as the scripture that follows in Matthew 12:44 describes a very disturbing scene. Matthew 12:44 KJV says, "*Then he saith, 'I will return to my house from which I came'; and when it comes, it finds it unoccupied, swept, and put in order.*" Basically, the place the spirit had left was cleaned and made ready to host a big fat demonic party.

Matthew 12:45 ESV states, "*Then it goes and brings with it seven other spirits more evil than itself, and they enter and dwell there, and the last state of that person is worse than the first. So also will it be with this evil generation.*" Imagine the nightmare situation of a house full of eight evil spirits worse than the first single spirit would be like? Such a situation no doubt is why so many people who live in a situation like that end up committing suicide, become junkies, or alcoholics just to escape the horrors they'd face from that kind of mad house.

Jezebel is not the only person to blame for what she would ultimately become. Her father and her people were the architects of just how screwed up she would become when she became the queen.[8] The Sidonians were a polytheistic

---

[8] Jezebel's father Ithobaal I was a priest-king from the temple of Astarte.

people that worshiped Baal just as the Israelites did when Jezebel came to power. What is not often seen though is that the Sidonians were more interested in the worship of goddesses than gods. Such reverence of the female deities is what helped to forge the image of Jezebel as a symbol of power and authority in an age where men normally held dominion.

CHAPTER 8: GODDESSES & QUEENS PART 1

There is a unique power that resonates with sound. The impact of sound on the human psyche is powerful and can be life changing. Sound is produced when something vibrates. Vibration can make or break material depending on how it is used.

Our brain is made up of billions of cells called neurons. Neurons use electricity to communicate with one another. They form into brain waves that create patterns. You can make two tones that are close together in frequency. The hearer's brain wave frequency will then fall into step with those frequencies. That is how sound vibrations can produce relaxation or healing at the cellular level. If you were to tap a glass and hear the frequency and then mimic the same frequency, the intensity of the sound vibration with the glass' own vibration will cause it to shatter. The speed of the sound waves through the air depends on how dense or far apart the particles are in the air.

Sound waves can travel faster through solid objects such as wood 13 times faster than in air, and 4 times faster in water than the air. Both sound and light travel together through the medium of waves. Light waves move freely through space. Sound waves being slower than light need a medium of transport. Moving light waves are electromagnetic waves. Within electromagnetic light waves exist radio waves. Within radio waves exists an even smaller range of waves that human beings can hear.

When God literally said 'Let there be light,' He was producing the beginning of sound. Things on the earth vibrate. Plants, rocks, and the earth itself vibrate with their own energy. Man however is different than other things. Because man is made in God's image, humans can make and release sound. Humans have the ability to release the sound of God. That type of ability with the gift of sound made and released by mankind can have negative effects if used improperly. Sadly, such an ability that allows humanity to release the sound (or sounds) of God in a negative manner does happen, and quite often.

Leaders often use sound to fulfill their goals. Many times they will use very negative sound waves instead of positive ones. Rulers of the ancient Middle East often pursued supernatural practitioners to further enhance their authority and power. One king of Israel name Manasseh did what was evil in the sight of the Lord. 2 Kings 21:3-6 ESV says:

"For he rebuilt the high places that Hezekiah his father had destroyed, and he erected altars for Baal and made an Asherah, as Ahab king of Israel had done, and worshipped all the host of heaven and served them. And he built altars in the house of the Lord, of which the Lord had said, "In Jerusalem will I put My name." And he built altars for all the host of heaven in the two courts of the house of the Lord. And he burned his son as an offering and used fortune telling and omens and dealt with mediums and with necromancers. He did much evil in the sight of the Lord, provoking Him to anger."

The sacrifice of Manasseh's son on the altar is sometimes described as going through the fire. As mentioned, going through the fire is referred to as the sacrifice to Moloch or the Moloch style of sacrifice.

Fire is an element that is associated with many things both

positive and negative. While fire is often associated with such notions as hell and damnation, it also has its roots in purity.

Fire is something that purifies. The book of Revelation states in Revelation 20:14 that hell and death will be thrown into the lake of fire. The lake of fire is called the second death. This is both scary and enticing because while one would not want to go to the lake of fire, there is finally an end to hell and death made through purification by the flames of the lake of fire.

The Lake of Fire is described in Revelation 19:20 as burning with sulfur. Revelation 20:15 ESV states, *"And if anyone's name was not found written in the book of life, he was thrown into the lake of fire."* This includes both men and women to be specific. Revelation 19:20 uses another interesting word aside from sulfur to describe being thrown into the lake of fire. Revelation 19:20 ESV says:

"And the beast was captured, and with it the false prophet who in its presence had done the signs by which he deceived those who had received the mark of the beast and those who worshiped its image. These two were thrown alive into the lake of fire that burn with sulfur."

The word *alive* is very important to grasp when you read Revelation 19:20. If the beast and false prophet are thrown into the lake of fire alive, then it is most likely anyone who is not mentioned in the Book of Life (also called the Lamb's Book of Life in reference to Jesus as the Lamb of God) is most likely going to be cast into the fire alive. That certainly is a frightening thought.

A young woman was interviewed in 2015 about a rare

medical chronic condition she suffers from as far back as childhood. Samara Rose suffers from two rare genetic conditions called Erythromegalia or Man on Fire Syndrome, and Renauld's syndrome. Erythomegalia leaves one feeling like they are experiencing constant second degree burns. Renauld's Syndrome leaves the body in a state of sensitivity to the slightest drop in temperature resulting in a terrible reaction when triggered. Samara says that any temperature other than seventeen degrees Celsius will lead her into "suffering."

Her disease is hereditary as she inherited it from her father who suffers from the same two conditions. Erythromegalia is a dysfunction of the thermal regulatory system that causes horrific nerve pain among other problems. The Renauld's syndrome causes a type of numbing burning pain when exposed to cooler temperatures. This example of suffering and horrific nerve pain is one of the best examples of constant "burning alive" descriptions that can be used for a very small observation of what it will be like for people in the lake of fire.

The entirety of the description of the lake of fire is spread throughout the Bible. Outside of the book of Revelation, the book of Matthew lists two specific scriptures about what awaits in the lake of fire. Matthew 13:50 ESV says, *"And throw them into the fiery furnace. In that place there will be weeping and gnashing of teeth."* The fiery furnace is a parable description for the lake of fire. The same mention of weeping and gnashing of teeth is mentioned in Matthew 8:12 ESV, *"While the sons of the kingdom of darkness will be thrown into the outer darkness. In that place there will weeping and gnashing of teeth."*

Here, the description of outer darkness is used. Matthew 25:46 ESV states, *"And these will go away into eternal punishment, but the righteous into eternal life."* The concept of punishment would invoke an idea of mental torment due to the mind dwelling on the constant aspect of guilt. All of the mentioning of weeping, gnashing of teeth, darkness, and punishment are examples of the physical and psychological sufferings that await in the lake of fire.

The lake of fire is something to be respected. It is something that shows God has created a place that will purify the elements of death and is a final destination for the evil that has corrupted life. Fire is a purifying force. That said, humanity and evil spirits have often taken fire and purification through fire to represent twisted and corrupt interpretations. The idea of how fire can make people suffer is replaced with the notion that it can please some god, goddess, or demon through the sacrifice of a person through fire and death.

Scriptural evidence found in Jude 1:12-13 gives an interesting description of elemental spirits in specific detail to function and where they are hidden. Jude 1:12-13 ESV says, *"These are hidden reefs at your love feasts, as they feast with you without fear, shepherds feeding themselves; waterless clouds, swept along by winds; fruitless trees in late autumn, twice dead, uprooted; wild waves of the sea, casting up the foam of their own shame; wandering stars, for whom the gloom of utter darkness has been reserved forever."* These verses are perhaps the first time Jude scriptures are seen in reference with elemental spirits.

Some scholars would perhaps argue that the scriptures refer to people instead of spirits, but it is the wording in the last sentence of the scripture of "wandering stars" and "the gloom of utter darkness has been reserved forever" that points to them being elemental spirits. This is backed up with the Jude 1:6 ESV scripture that states, *"And the angels who did not stay within their own position of authority, but left their proper dwelling, He has kept in eternal chains under gloomy darkness until the judgment of the great day."* The difference in the darkness descriptions with the words *utter* and *gloomy* point to the differences in the types of spirits already in chains in darkness, and those that will one day be put in chains and eternal darkness.

Elements are associated with nature. Nature worship and uses for magic are the basis for Wiccan. Nature is the roots for witchcraft. While witchcraft is a broad term that varies societally and culturally, the application of natural elements is often essential in the practice.

Next to nature, the driving force behind witchcraft is magic. Magic is defined as the power of influencing the course of events by using mysterious or superstitious forces. One who practices magic is summarized as having or apparently having supernatural powers. Practitioners of magic are able or move, change, or to create by or as if by magic (referring to illusion). There are several types of practitioners of magic. Among magic practices or arts are sorcery, witchcraft, wizardry, necromancy, enchantment, voodoo, hoodoo, mojo, shamanism, and other styles that deal with magic in a variety of fields.

It is important to understand that no two users of magic are the same. It is like trying to identify a Satanist as a Luciferian, or vice versa. Luciferianism is a belief system that venerates the essential characteristics that are affixed to Lucifer. Satanism is a group of ideological and philosophical beliefs based on Satan.

Satanists and Luciferians regard Satan as their main focus and center for worship. However, both groups have very different beliefs, views, philosophies, and practices. To say that one is the same as the other is shear stupidity. One who tries to take someone out of such groups and doesn't understand such differences will usually fail at their task of saving the life of a member of either group. They will not be ready for the battle ahead as they will not have the correct knowledge of what it is they are dealing with or about to engage with for ones deliverance.

2 Corinthians 6:14 ESV says, *"Do not be unequally yoked with unbelievers. For what partnership has righteousness with lawlessness? Or what fellowship has light with darkness?"* It pays off in the end to know exactly what you are dealing with when studying things of the supernatural, elements of the occult, or anything paranormal. Many people today just throw everything in one basket and call it whatever they want in order to save time. Those people always pay the price in the end. Ignorance is not bliss when it comes to standing and winning in spiritual warfare

There is a big difference between a witch, sorcerer, and magician. The Bible lists these magic users in very different categories for the sole reason of making sure that people know they are different. Different spiritual elements go into all of the practices and beliefs of each practitioner. Luke 16:13 ESV states, *"No servant can serve two masters, for either he will hate the one and love the other, or he will be devoted to the one and*

*Hecate, or The Night of Enitharmon's Joy. A William Blake
Painting of Hecate the Greek Goddess of Witchcraft and Death
Surrounded by Nature. Courtesy of Eloquence.*

despise the other. You cannot serve God and money."

All elements of magic that are outside the realm of illusion
and tricks are associated with the supernatural. Magic users
often try practicing some form of interaction with a type of

spirit or spirits. As mentioned, the supernatural is very attractive to people. That is because the supernatural is filled with many elements of the unknown. People may be afraid of what is not known, but they are even more afraid of not attempting to learn the things not known to them.

Referring back to the nature of sound is an important aspect to understand about hearing and receiving. Words are fueled by belief, devotion, and conviction. A word spoken with intensity that fuels what is said can be a powerful motivation for a listener. Throughout the world are vast movements that are compelled by people who have the tools to attain followers. What makes them gain a following is found in the substances that their messages are laced with under the skin.

Often, the means of gaining followers for a movement is based on three things. Those things are as follows:

1. **Spectacle- a visually striking performance, display, event, or scene regarded in terms for its visual impact. People love to be entertained and impressed. When a message has a bit of flare and drama tied in then people will pay more attention.**

2. **Theme- The subject matter of a talk, piece of writing, a person's thoughts, topic, or an exhibition that can be given a particular setting or ambience for such as a venue or activity. People like a good story tied into the subject in which they are learning. what they are learning. It makes for a more alluring pull to what**

someone is learning about.

3. **Hype- to stimulate, agitate, or excite with flamboyant or dramatic methods for promotion or publicity. Sporting event promoters usually will use hype to sell a fight to gain more viewers, ratings, and purchasing of tickets and pay-per-views. The more hyping of an event, the more millions of dollars it can make.**

People love a good show. In today's age everybody loves to be entertained with a huge spectacle event that is spruced up with a great theme and promoted heavily with a lot of hype behind it. Superstars are born because of such promotions. In the ancient world religions and cults were no less the same in terms of using spectacle, theme, and hype for the promotion and seizing of power.

Most of the ancient world was influenced by three particular civilizations. Those three were Egypt, Mesopotamia, and the Steppe cultures of Eurasia. Egypt is considered to be the birthplace of magic. Mesopotamia is considered the inspiration for many of the religious deities that other cultures would take and adopt for their own purposes throughout the copper, bronze, and iron ages. The Steppe cultures contributed to the rise of many religious themes spread through the Middle East, Aegean, and Eastern European cultures by their worship of and reverence for fire and other elements such as water.

Psalm 104:4 ESV says, *"He makes His messengers winds, His ministers a flaming fire."* Fire is one of the most powerful symbols used throughout all the cultures, histories, and

122

religions of the entire world. Fire is associated with the energy of life. It is a necessary destructive force that brings about new life. Fire is destructive and creative, dangerous and desirable, threatening and necessary. Fire in conjunction with spiritual entities such as what is described in Psalm 104:4 creates a very powerful force of awe and control.

The Steppe civilizations developed one of the very first religions called Zoroastrianism. Known also as Mazdayasna, Zoroastrianism is an extant religion combining cosmogonic dualism and eschatological monotheism in a manner that is unique among the major religions of the world. Attributed to creation by the Iranian prophet Zoroaster (Zarahustra), the deity known as Ahura Mazda is the supreme being or god of the Zoroastrian faith. The religion believes in heaven and hell, free will, messianism, and has influence on the three great world religions of the modern age in Christianity, Judaism, and Islam.

Zoroastrianism is known most for its reverence of fire. Known as *atar* in Zoroastrianism, fire is a sacred symbol of being the visible presence of Ahura Mazda (the creator god) and his *asha* or importance. Zoroastrian worshipers have built fire temples to house their atar holy fires. Theses temples have a fire that burns day and night to represent purity.

While not practiced today, pre-Zoroastrian beliefs viewed fire as a medium or faculty through which judgments could be rendered by having ordeals by the heart or trials by fire. The belief was that if someone passes the fiery test through blazing, shining, and molten metal, then they would have attained physical and spiritual strength, wisdom, truth, love,

Zoroastrian Eternal Flame Courtesy of Adam Jones, PHD.

and serenity. It is estimated that there have been thirty trials by fire tests in the history of Zoroastrianism all together.

The mention of Zoroastrianism is for their use of fire as a way to purify them by passing through the fire. 1 Corinthians

3:13 ESV states, *"Each one's work will become manifest, for the day will disclose it, because it will be revealed by fire, and the fire will test what sort of work each one has done.* Then, 1 Corinthians 3:15 ESV says, *"If anyone's work is burned up, he will suffer loss, though he himself will be saved, but only as through fire."* Fire, by how God has defined it, is the best way of truly testing something or someone to see if they are true or false, good or bad, truthful or lying, pure or wicked, and so on.

God's views of fire are not usually literal, though some occasions have called for literal uses of fire for testing and tribulation. No, God has more metaphorical uses of fire for testing a person's heart, profession, and worth. The fire is the spiritual fire that God uses, as He Himself is fire. Hebrews 12:29 ESV declares, *"For our God is a consuming fire."* If God is fire, and His messengers are made to be fire, then there will always be some form of fire involved in the trials of the spirit.

Sound can be a powerful method of trial by fire. James 3:6 ESV says, *"And the tongue is a fire, a world of unrighteousness. The tongue is set among our members, staining the whole body, setting on fire the entire course of life, and set on fire by hell."* The state of Israel during the time of Jezebel had become burned up by a flame from her words and practices. What makes Jezebel so unique among all the leaders, both foreign and domestic, was the fact that she was quite possibly a practicing witch.

Jezebel came from the Phoenicians. The Phoenicians descended from the Canaanites. Sidon was a Phoenician city-state. The Sidonians had become a people that adopted different cultures and practices and merged them into their society for their own imagery purposes. They had continued the practices of the Canaanite religions in their society, but had also evolved to include other cultural aspects including the use of magic. In conclusion, they had evolved into a civilization of witches and witchcraft.

CHAPTER 9: GODDESSES & QUEENS PART 2

One of the biggest cultures the Phoenicians took elements from and adopted for their own society was Egypt. Egypt is considered the mother of magic. This is in reference to the elements of magic that the Egyptians believed in and applied to their daily lives. Their chief gods and deities who were involved in magic were primarily female.

Exodus 7:11 ESV says *"Then Pharaoh summoned the wise men and the sorcerers, and they, the magicians of Egypt, also did the same by their secret arts."* The Egyptians were heavily into magic. They formed cults around particular gods and goddesses that required rituals and sacrifices that were shrouded in secrecy.

The holy book of the Egyptians called *The Book of the Dead* or *Coming Forth by Day* (the original title) is actually a spell book designed to help keep the dead safe as they traveled through the underworld to paradise. It should be noted that the Book of the Dead is not a spell book like a witches *Grimoire* or *Book of Shadows*. The difference is the Book of the Dead is full of spells for the dead to use to aid in navigating through dangerous areas and fending off demons, while a witches Book of Shadows is designed for use in the living world to perform enchantments, curses, necromancy, and other little things.[9]

Egypt had a strong male dominated society. However, it is likely that women over the centuries were powerful influencers behind the scenes. Women in Egypt were revered

---

[9] Necromancy- supposed practice of communicating with the dead, especially in order to predict the future.

both socially and religiously. One not so often viewpoint of ancient Egypt is the "gender" of the animal deities that the Egyptians worshiped and held in reverence. The Vulture, for example, is a bird that represented matriarchal stratum or leadership. It was a bird that represented the Pharaohs and was placed in depictions of the great kings of Egypt. What is interesting however is the vulture actually was female instead of male. The kings of a male dominated society used a female emblem for their roles as leaders.

The Sidonians from which Jezebel came were made up of two Sidons. Each one was under the leadership of kings that had adopted ways of life from other cultures and civilizations. They adopted and assimilated ways of life to formulate a society based on the methods similar to their ways of business that the Phoenicians had mastered.

The Phoenicians were what can be described as the Switzerland of the ancient world. They were basically a banking state that had made amazing strides throughout the known world at the time of their placing on the map. By around 1250 B.C. Phoenician merchants had learned to navigate by the stars at night. They had learned to use the North Star as a fixed point in the sky. The Phoenicians were also the first to circumnavigate around Africa according to various Greek sources. They built some of the best ships at the time due to their lumber and cedar trees from Lebanon.

The Phoenicians developed the first known global alphabet. With a 22 letter based system with no vowels but a sound for every symbol, the countries the Phoenicians traveled to adopt and used their alphabet system. The idea of different sounds of speech being able to be written using a system of 30 or less letters originated from the Phoenician alphabet.

The Phoenicians had trading posts all over the ancient world in such places as Carthage, Cadiz, Cyprus, and Rhodes. They traded in everything from cedar wood, ivory, wine, embroidered cloth, pottery, metal, and even wood carvings. The Phoenicians were famous for making purple dye from a rock called Tyrian Purple. The dye was an exquisite fashion accessory. The Phoenician name the Greeks gave them actually means purple men due to their skills in purple dye.

Crafting was one of the bigger parts of Phoenician culture. They were very skilled at glass making. The technique of free blowing for glass making came from the Phoenicians. The ivory trade that the modern world frowns upon due to ivory coming from endangered animals such as elephants was a major source of income for the Phoenicians. Ivory carving was a great skill of the Phoenicians and a second source of income for them. They could craft anything such as chairs, footstools, thrones, and beds from Ivory.

The greatest accomplishment that the Phoenicians are known for throughout the world is the alphabet. As mentioned, the 22-letter system that the Phoenician merchants used in their travels were adopted by nearly everyone that came into contact with them. Without the Phoenician alphabet, reading and writing would not be what it is today.[10] The accomplishments of the Phoenicians were

---

[10] Interesting side note is that the modern day numerical system of most western and eastern countries came from the Middle East by way of Saudi Arabia's ancestors who created Arabic Numbers. In short, letters and numbers of today would not be what they are without help from the Middle East.

Bull Protome (adornment or decoration) of Persian influence From Sidon Courtesy of Eli+.

what would lead the Sidonians into both blessings and curses during the reign of Jezebel.

The expansion of Phoenicia gave the people access to all sorts of cultures that had many different religions, beliefs, and a wide variety of cults. It would not be hard to surmise that many of these cults commissioned the craftsmen of Phoenicia to make idols and images that they would worship in their day-to-day lives. It is most plausible that a vice versa situation arose where the Phoenicians, especially the Sidonians, began to worship those same images or at the least be influenced by them.

1 Corinthians 8:4-5 KJV states, *"As concerning therefore the eating of those things that are offered in sacrifice unto idols, we know that an idol is nothing in the world, and that there is none other God but one. For though there be that are called gods, whether in heaven or in earth, (as there be gods many, and lords many)..."*

Both foreign gods and their own gods from their ancestors of Canaan influenced the Sidonians. The Canaanite religions had evolved into the Phoenician religions that Jezebel would use to dominate the Israelites during her reign. While the Israelites were aware of a single all-powerful God in Yahweh, that didn't mean that they couldn't be led astray. Many Israelites accepted the religions of the Sidonians either by forced religious oppression or willing acceptance due to actual belief in Baal and Astarte.

Many of the cult pursuits that the Sidonians pursued were based on astrology, necromancy, and nature worship. Amos 5:8 ESV says, *"He who made the Pleiades and Orion, and turns the deep darkness into the morning and darkens the day into night, who calls for the waters of the sea and pours them out on the surface of the earth, the LORD is His name."*

The mention of this scripture in Amos is important because of the identification of the two star constellations that are mentioned. The Pleiades and Orion are vastly significant to star worshipers of the ancient world. Many of the gods and goddesses that Sidon adopted into their religious practices were associated with stars and planets.

Orion is known as a prominent constellation located on the celestial equator. It is visible throughout the entire world. It is one of the most recognizable and conspicuous constellations of the night sky. The Pleiades is an open star cluster containing middle-aged B-type hot stars. The Pleiades is among the closest star clusters to Earth. It is the star cluster most obvious to be seen by the naked eye in the night sky.

Aside from the Biblical scriptures, there is a Greek myth that connects the Orion and Pleiades. After the Titan Atlas was forced to carry the heavens on his shoulders (the sky in some translations), Orion (a mighty hunter in Greek mythology) began to pursue all of the Pleiades who were the seven daughters of Atlas. Zeus transformed them into doves and later into stars to comfort their father so they wouldn't be caught by Orion who was said to still be in pursuit of the Pleiades. Orion was a demi-god in Greek mythology. Many Greek demi-gods were possibly Nephilim. Nephilim are the sons and daughters of angels and humans. Nephilim have a connection to goddess cults and witchcraft through their reverence for Venus.

The Pleiades and Orion are mentioned along side two planets in the Bible. Venus and Saturn are mentioned by different names in the Bible along side their current names that are used in Astronomy. Amos 5:26 KJV states, *"But ye have borne the tabernacle of your Moloch and Chiun your images, the star of your god, which ye made to yourselves."*

Chiun is identified as Saturn. Saturn was considered by

132

ancient astrologers as baleful in influence.[11] The Phoenicians offered human sacrifices to Saturn, especially children sacrifices. Saturn is the representation of Cronus (Cronus is named Saturn by the Romans when they mixed and matched planets and the Greek pantheon together). If Moloch is indeed a ritual sacrifice rather than a god to the Phoenicians, then one can see a deeper connection to Greek influence on Phoenician culture.

Venus is a little more diverse in it's mentioning. Isaiah 14:12 ESV says, *"How you are fallen from heaven, O Day Star, son of Dawn! How you are cut down to the ground, you who laid the nations low!"* The Isaiah scripture normally is referring to Lucifer as the morning star. However, there has been belief that Venus is actually the representation of Lucifer in certain theological circles. Venus is considered the morning and evening star because it can appear from Earth up to 47 degrees away from the Sun. During the times it can be seen when it is rising or setting a few hours before or after the Sun, Venus can be seen just before sunrise or after sunset as a bright morning or evening star.

The Hebrew word for Lucifer is Helel, but the actual translation is still being interpreted. The Isaiah 14:12 verse also has been known to use in certain translations the name Helel Ben Shahar, which is called the king of Babylon in some text readings. The Babylonians were star worshipers and had a strong tie-in to Venus through their goddesses. While interesting in theory, the Isaiah 14:12 scripture is very controversial for anything other than an interesting point of

---

[11] Baleful-threatening harm; menacing.

observation. The actual scripture that mentions Venus is found in Jeremiah 44:17.

Jeremiah 44:17 ESV says, *"But we will do everything that we have vowed, make offerings to the queen of heaven and pour out drink offerings to her, as we did, both we and our fathers, our kings and our officials, in the cities of Judah and in the streets of Jerusalem. For then we had plenty of food, and prospered, and saw no disaster."*

The queen of heaven is Venus. Saturn and Venus are thought of in two particular ways. Saturn is considered as primeval unity, creator, and a central sun when heaven was close to earth. Venus is viewed as a star of glory, a mother goddess, and a great comet.

Like Venus, The Babylonians also revered Saturn as Shamash. The same way that one side of the moon always faces earth, the north pole of Saturn with its hexagon star-like design was fixed in the sky facing Earth. It had a polar alignment with Earth's north pole. Saturn could be seen as a star similar to the sun with eight rays similar to the star of Ishtar. Both Shamash and Ishtar are seen as brother and sister therefore making Saturn and Venus siblings in Babylonian historical culture. The connecting points of Saturn and Venus with Jezebel and witchcraft have to do with Saturn being associated with human sacrifice, and Venus being associated with "chaos magic."

Chaos magic, also spelled magick, is defined as a contemporary magical practice that emphasizes the pragmatic use of belief systems and the creation of new and unorthodox methods. The combination of human sacrifice, religious fervor, and witchcraft created a powerful force of chaos that

Star of Shamash, Similar to Star of Ishtar But With 4 Waves Instead of Points Points Courtesy of Gryffindor.

would ring or thread throughout the Phoenician kingdoms during the reign of Jezebel and other members of her family both male and female. The gods and goddesses that the Phoenicians worshiped had another unique and chaotic part to them.

The gods and goddesses that the Phoenicians worshiped had dual representations of gender. What this means is that gods could sometimes become goddesses and vice-versa. Not only was this common among Phoenicians, but also among Egyptian, Levantine, Persian Gulf, and Steppe culture pantheons. Greek civilization didn't use a duality system like eastern cultures did in terms of males sometimes appearing female or females appearing male. However, there was a strong emphasize on sexual preference among the Greek pantheons of gods and goddesses that was more homosexual and bisexual in nature. An example of this is in the stories of the Greek God Zeus lusting after and having sexual relations with both men and women.

Sexual practices such as orgies and mass homosexuality were a common practice among witches. One primary connecting factor between the Jezebel spirit, witchcraft, and homosexuality is domination. Jezebel was a dominating and intimidating woman. Dominating people can often take advantage of weaker individuals such as those that have suffered from a tragedy or as heartbreak.

Heartbreak usually carries six symptoms with it in the form of insomnia, digestive problems, mental fog, sensitivity to illness, headaches, and physical heartache. Insomnia can lead to depression and anxiety. Mental fog can be created from stress, insomnia, and emotional turmoil. All of these symptoms can be targets of spirits that want to be in control of those weaker than themselves.

A Jezebel spirit is often manifested through abuse. People who have suffered from abuse often seek to gain control of their own lives through the application of control. Control can sometimes appear in the form of hurting others similar to how bullies pick on people as bullies can sometimes be victims suffering from abuse and seek to take out their anger on other people.

A spirit is as different as a human body. The spirit can manifest feminine and masculine types of spirits. It is due to the nature of which a spirit is manifested. Men and women live vastly different lives.

While men and women can at times take on the same roles as one another, there is still a vast level of difference between each gender physically, mentally, and spiritually. That said, the same types of masculine and feminine spirits could affect men and women. Spirits are not necessarily gendered without a human host. Rather, they can appear or affect a body (human) depending on the purpose of the manifestation or possession. The interesting part is what happens after such occurrences transpire. One such example of different spiritual manifestations can be seen in the study and examination of the duality of the Holy Spirit or what is called Shekinah.

CHAPTER 10: THE DUAL NATURE OF SHEKINAH

1 Corinthians 11:7 ESV states, *"For a man should not wear anything on his head when worshiping, for man is made in God's image and reflects God's glory. And woman reflects man's glory."* Women are a symbol of glory. Men have valued women as a symbol of glory throughout history. Women have always been highly favored as items and trophies of glory in many stories.

The story in *The Illiad* of the war between the Greeks and Trojans was due to the desire to possess Helen of Troy as a trophy because of her beauty. King David in the Bible cursed his own family with his actions of desiring to possess Bathsheba, who belonged to the loyal soldier Urijah. King Solomon is famous in the Bible for his interactions with women whom he wrote great love songs and poetry, which was extensive when you consider he had over 1,000 wives and concubines. Oddly enough he didn't really like any of them as Ecclesiastes 7:28 ESV reads, *"Which my soul has sought repeatedly, but I have not found. One man among a thousand I found, but a woman among all these I have not found."*

The feminine quality of women has always been the greatest of attractions to men. The masculine side of man is made whole from the feminine side of woman as it is something that has been absent from man since the day Eve was separated through the side of Adam and formed into woman. Man has sought to make himself whole with that indwelling feeling they get from a woman who is that one special person a man longs for in his life. They are the indwelling glory that a man longs to have inside of them.

The indwelling glory a man receives from a woman that

makes him feel whole is the same feeling that the Holy Spirit gives those who receives Him into their lives. The Holy Spirit is the indwelling presence of God the Father. He is the One who gave Jesus His authority to perform miracles on the Earth. The Holy Spirit is the glory of God that man can receive when they ask Him to come over them, anoint them, and be in with them. John 14:17 ESV states, *"Even the Spirit of truth, whom the world cannot receive, because it neither sees Him nor knows Him. You know Him, for He dwells with you and will be with in you."*

The Holy Spirit is described as the glory of God in some accounts of Him in the Bible. Isaiah 60:2 ESV says, *"For behold, darkness shall cover the earth, and thick darkness the peoples; but the Lord will arise upon you, and his glory will be seen upon you."* Luke 2:9 ESV states, *"And an angel of the Lord appeared to them, and the glory of the Lord shone around them, and they were filled with great fear."*

The Luke 2:9 scripture is describing the birth of Jesus and the appearing of the angel before the shepherds who were tending to their sheep. It is likely that the glory of God that was shone around them was the coming of the Holy Spirit perhaps to share in the celebration of the birth of Jesus due to the description of a multitude of the heavenly host appearing and celebrating. Another scripture found in Romans 9:4 NLV reads, *"They are the people of Israel, chosen to be God's adopted children. God revealed His glory to them. He made covenants with them and gave them His law. He gave them the privilege of worshiping Him and receiving His wonderful promises."*

God gave mankind His glory to make a more fulfilled image of God. Mankind is made in the image of God. It is only fitting that God complete His image with the same indwelling 'spirit and glory' that surrounds Him. Jesus represented that image on earth. Matthew 17:5 ESV says, *"He was still speaking when, behold, a bright cloud overshadowed them, and a voice from the cloud said, "This is My beloved Son, with whom I am well pleased, listen to Him."* The cloud is the representation of Shekinah. Shekinah is defined as "that which dwells." Shekinah comes from the Hebrew verb shaken (shakhan) that means "to dwell or reside." Shekinah is one name for the Holy Spirit or Spirit of God.

Shekinah is not a masculine name. Rather, the name Shekinah is feminine in nature. The Holy Spirit is described as a "He" in the Bible. But, the Holy Spirit is more than just the persona of a man, or even just another representation of God. The Holy Spirit is "God's Glory."

Another way to define Shekinah it that is denotes the divine presence of God. It is the feminine aspect of Divinity or the Divine Presence. The word Shekinah is often used to refer to birds' nesting or to a bird's nest. The use of Shekinah with birds is to show that birds dwell with or near those of its kind. The divine presence of God resides with those that are similar to it like humans who are made in God's image.

The Hebrew word for tabernacle, *mikshan,* is a derivative of the same root word as Shekinah for dwelling place. Mikshan is found in the Bible in Psalms 132:5 ESV, *"Until I find a place for the Lord, a dwelling place for the Mighty One of Jacob."*

Numbers 24:5 NIV also reads, *"How beautiful are your tents, Jacob, your dwelling places, Israel!"* In classical Jewish thought, Shekinah is a reference to a dwelling or settling of divine presence that in proximity to the Shekinah, when the connection to God is more readily perceived. This can be seen in similarity with Matthew 18:20 ESV where it says, *"For where two or more are gathered in My name, there am I among them."*

Drawing from parallels of Solomon's Temple and the Tabernacle where the Spirit of God rested in the Holy of Holies, the same can also be said of the Spirit of God resting in the hearts of mankind. John 17:22 ESV says, *"The glory that You have given Me I have given to them, that they may be one even as We are one."* Shekinah is linked to prophecy in Judaism. The Holy Spirit is the bringer of prophecy in the Old and New Testament. 2 Peter 1:21 ESV states, *"For no prophecy was ever produced by the will of man, but men spoke from God as they were carried along by the Holy Spirit."*

Oracles in the ancient world such as those found in ancient Greece and Egypt were often women. Fortunetellers in the Bible such as those possessed by demons were often young women that could predict the future. One Bible example is that of a young woman the Apostle Paul encountered in Acts 16:16 who accurately predicted that he was a man of God (Paul would later cast the demon out of her).

The young woman Paul encountered made her owners a lot of money for the predictions she made. It could be theorized that other women oracles were possessed by demons or spirits similar to how the young woman of Acts 16:16. King Leonidas of the legendary 300 Spartans of Thermopylae visited an oracle before his battle that predicted either Greece would fall to the Persians or he would have to

Picture of a Rock Dove. The Dove is a Symbol of the Holy Spirit. Courtesy of Alan D. Wilson.

die to secure the future of the Greeks.

Prediction is defined as a forecast, a statement of an uncertain event, or the expectation of future behavior. A prediction is not a hundred percent known, but can be surmised to happen based on facts presented which seem to give a solid final estimate of probability that something can and will happen. Prophecy is defined as something that is told to someone by God or a god. It is something that is divinely inspired, interpreted, or revealed by divine insight of events to come. In short, a prediction is a surmising of something that could happen, while a prophecy is something that will happen.

The Holy Spirit is more than just the bringer of true future events. He is God just as Jesus is God. He is a member of the Holy Trinity of the God Head. One of the names of God, *Elohim,* is a plural name for gods. The Holy Spirit is the glory of God that is what brings God's anointing to humanity. It is a great honor to receive the glory of God. Angels long to have a relationship with the Holy Spirit like humans have.

1 Peter 1:12 ESV says, *"It was revealed to them that they were serving not themselves but you, in the things that have now been announced to you through those who preached the good news to you by the Holy Spirit sent from heaven, things into which angels long to look."* Angels must earn the anointing of the Holy Spirit just like humans receive the Holy Spirit as a gift from God. Angels can have anointing like Lucifer who was described as the "anointed cherub." Ezekiel 28:14 ESV states, *"You were an anointed guardian cherub. I placed you; you were on the holy mountain of God; in the midst of the stones of fire you walked."*

The word 'anoint' is defined as to ceremonially confer divine or holy office upon, to consecrate, bless, ordain, or crown for authority. To be anointed is to have a high honor placed upon one's shoulders. Angels who have the anointing of the Holy Spirit have been given one of the highest honors that God can give. They would be given the glory of God just as Lucifer was given before his fall from grace.

The Holy Spirit is depicted as a dove in symbolism and in physical description. Luke 3:22 ESV states, *"and the Holy Spirit descended on him in bodily form, like a dove; and a voice came from heaven, "You are My beloved Son; with You I am well pleased."* Jesus received both the glory of God and the authority of God. He had been anointed as king and high priest by his cousin John the Baptist, a Levite by birth and the son of the priest Zechariah. John had baptized Jesus with water, but the Holy Spirit had baptized Him with fire.

Matthew 3:11 ESV states, *"I baptize you with water for repentance, but he who is coming after me is mightier than I, whose sandals I am not worthy to carry. He will baptize you with the Holy Spirit and fire."*

John the Baptist was describing the difference between his method of baptizing (baptizing is the act of making sanctified) with water in the natural, and the supernatural baptism that would happen when the Holy Spirit and Jesus would come to live inside the heart of someone who accepted them. Here in the above scripture in Matthew 3:11, Jesus would actually be baptized with the fire of the Holy Spirit. Jesus did this in order to show mankind what John was talking about as made evident when He was baptized first by water, then had the Holy Spirit or Shekinah come over Him. Jesus was sanctified with water, and then purified with fire by the Holy Spirit.

Referring for a moment back to Zoroastrianism, there is actually a second element that is just as important as fire in the religion. Water or *Aban* in Zoroastrianism in league with fire or *Atar* are agents of ritual purity. Fire and water are accepted as both agents of sanctification and purification.

Psalm 66:10-12 ESV says, *"For you, O God, have tested us; you have tried us as a silver is tried. You brought us into the net; you laid a crushing burden on our backs; you let men ride over our heads; we went through fire and through water; yet you have brought us out to a place of abundance."*

In metallurgy, the process of making a very good sword is done when steel is heated with fire, and then cooled with water. It is the duality of two elements that are different yet working hand in hand to make the greatest out of something by coming full circle. This means that two things can make something complete, fulfilled, and true. Using fire and water in the baptism of Jesus was a way to anoint Him as king and high priest. It further allowed the Holy Spirit to come make Jesus complete as the "Last Adam."

When the female was taken from the side of "man" and was formed into a second body, we can see that Adam, in a sense, was incomplete as a complete or whole man. His wife Eve completed him as his companion and spouse, but only through the act of Adam accepting her into his heart and thus completing him through the joining of man and woman. The Holy Spirit coming to dwell in Jesus is a different but fulfilling approach to the same kind of joining of man and woman in the heart. 1 Corinthians 15:45 ESV states, *"Thus it is written, "The first man Adam became a living being"; the last Adam became a life-giving spirit."* Observe the phrase "life-giving spirit." Genesis 3:20 ESV says, *"The man called his wife's name Eve, because she was the mother of all living."* Eve was the giver of life because she could birth life. The Holy Spirit is the bringer of "complete life" or complete living.

2 Corinthians 3:6 ESV says, *"Who made us sufficient to be ministers of a new covenant, not of the letter but of the Spirit. For the letter kills, but the Spirit gives life."* Then, 1 Corinthians 2:11 ESV reads, *"For who knows a person's thoughts except the spirit of that person, which is in him? So also no one comprehends the thoughts of God except the Spirit of God."*

The Holy Spirit lives inside God. He is the voice of God that works with mankind to make humanity a complete creation in God. John 1:1-5 ESV states, *"In the beginning was the Word, and the Word was with God, and the Word was God. He was in the beginning with God. All things were made through Him, and without Him was not anything made that was made. In Him was life, and the life was the light of men. The light shines in the darkness, and the darkness has not overcome it."*

The New Living Translation of John 1:4 says, *"The Word gave life to everything that was created, and His life brought light to everyone."* The Word is the Holy Spirit. The Holy Spirit is the living voice of God manifested through the entirety of the John 1:1-5 scriptures. It makes a complete and perfect picture of God the Father, Jesus the Son, and the Holy Ghost as the "Living Word." This truly depicts three in one.

John 4:24 ESV reads, *"God is spirit, and those who worship Him must worship in spirit and truth."* The Holy Spirit is the Spirit of God and the word of truth. Together they form a perfect circle of completion of Shekinah and *Ruach Hakodesh*. Ruach Hakodesh is a Hebrew name for the Holy Spirit that means "Divine Inspiration." It is the inspiration through which attuned individuals perceive and use what is given by the Holy Spirit to them for purposes of action, writing, or speech. This is how the Holy Spirit imparts prophecy to those who He sees as worthy to receive the gifts of seeing a true and absolute future that will happen unlike a prediction where it may or may not happen.

The joining of Shekinah and Ruach Hakodesh is similar to the oneness of men and women. Mark 10:6-9 ESV says, *"But from the beginning of creation, 'God made them male and female. Therefore a man shall leave his father and mother and hold fast to his wife, and the two shall become one flesh.' So they are no longer two but one flesh. What therefore God has joined together, let not man separate."*

Like a man with a woman, mankind can't be without the Holy Spirit when they receive Him. It is like a great void that can't be filled by anything else. Psalm 51:11 ESV states, *"Cast me not away from your presence, and take not your Holy Spirit from me."* Then, Isaiah 63:10-11 ESV reads, *"But they rebelled and grieved His Holy Spirit; therefore He turned to be their enemy, and*

Himself fought against them. Then He remembered the days of old, of Moses and his people. Where is He who brought them up out of the sea with the shepherds of His flock? Where is He who put in the midst of them His Holy Spirit…"

These two scriptures are where the possessive form of Ruach Hakodesh is used in the Bible. They give excellent definition and meaning of Ruach Hakodesh. In other forms, Ruach Hakodesh is considered the divine force and influence of God over His creations, the universe, and life itself.

The Holy Spirit is seen as a teacher. Psalm 51:13 ESV says, *"Then I will teach transgressors your ways, and sinners will return to you."* The Holy Spirit acts like a mother in a lot of ways similar to how God is the father. A mother teaches, raises, and rears her children in the ways of correct thinking and action. The Holy Spirit teaches and raises the children of God in the ways of righteousness. Jesus called the Holy Spirit a "helper" and "helpmate."

Mankind himself is not righteous. However, the Holy Spirit is God's way of helping mankind walk in the steps of righteousness. He helps mankind to walk in the ways of God rather than on a path to God. A path to God is created by mankind to find their own way such as through self-righteousness, religion, and rules that mankind creates to "get to heaven." Acts 4:12 ESV says, *"And there is no salvation in no one else, for there is no other name under heaven given among men by which we must be saved."*

A way to God is the correct way to Him as made evident by when people accept Jesus as John 14:6 ESV states, *"Jesus answered, "I am the way, the truth, and the life. No one comes to the Father except through Me."* Jesus is the way to God verified in John 6:44 ESV which reads, *"No one can come to me unless the Father who sent me draws him. And I will raise him up on the last day."* One must always follow the way to God instead of a path to be with Him.

2 Corinthians 3:17 ESV reads, *"Now the Lord is the Spirit, and where the Spirit of the Lord is, there is freedom."* The Holy Spirit is freedom in God. He is the release of the burdens from the shoulders of people to truly enter into a full completion of who someone is in God and Christ Jesus. It is available to both men and women as the Holy Spirit represents both masculine and feminine completion in God just as mankind becomes whole through the joining of man and woman. God made mankind in His image, but completed the picture of man through His Son with the fullness of the Spirit of God that comes to dwell in the hearts of mankind as He did with Jesus.

The duality of male and female traits that are found in the Holy Spirit is to show that the Spirit of God does not discern a difference between the two sexes. In God's view, both are one as they came out of a man but became separate only to be rejoined again in a more fulfilled capacity. No longer 'one by design, but 'one' by choice. There are physical manifestations of male and female angels, spirits, and demons, but the Holy Spirit is above all those things.

The Holy Spirit is the indwelling presence of God that makes men and women complete and 'one' in the eyes of God. Galatians 3:20 ESV states, *"Now an intermediary implies more than one, but God is one."* Just as God is one with Jesus the Son and the Holy Spirit, God also views male and female as one. To Him, the only difference is the individuality of each person. God made every man and woman fearfully and wonderfully made. This is the true meaning of equality that God longs to see in His human creation. The equality of a complete image of God that humanity is made to represent as His image with the indwelling of the Holy Spirit.

CHAPTER 11: MAGIC & WITCH QUEENS

Just as prophecy is associated with the Holy Spirit, predictions are associated with other types of spirits. Predictions made by man are their way of trying to foretell the future through particular circumstances and possible outcomes that depend on certain kinds of evidence to promote a probable outcome of a future possibly happening as predicted. Predictions are therefore a spiritual and scientific observation that mankind has endeavored to practice and pursue. Scientific prediction is based on fact finding.

Acts 17:11 ESV says, *"Now these Jews were more noble than those in Thessalonica; they received the word with all eagerness, examining the scriptures daily to see if these things were so."* In the scientific application of predicting future events, examination of evidence is required. Examining facts, evidence, and pieces of information are essential to making a reasonable surmising of a possible future outcome. It is a way to properly predict something through the application of wisdom and knowledge mixed with understanding the complete or near complete and total meaning of evidence presented for knowing the future. Predictions made through the realm of the Holy Spirit are a completely different matter.

Revelation 16:14 ESV states, *"For they are demonic spirits, performing signs, who go abroad to the kings of the whole world, to assemble them for battle on the great day of God the Almighty."* The realm of the supernatural is filled with all kinds of spirits. Some are of God, some are of the devil, and some are neither associated with either God or Satan. Many people never realize that the realm of the spirit is vast and has hordes of beings that simply do what they desire and not for someone in authority over them. These spirits are negative and dark, but they serve their own ends different than what most of mankind has been taught in small dogmatic and narrow-minded viewpoints. Only when people are shown a much more broad and scriptural based examination of the supernatural realm will mankind be able to properly deal with such spirits that come against humanity.

Matthew 24:24 ESV says, *"For false Christ's and false prophets will arise and perform great signs and wonders, so as to lead astray, if possible, even the elect."* Spirits manifest in many different people through manipulation, suggestion, possession, and influence. The practitioners of certain forms of magic use all sorts of methods to arouse people to come into their fold and be manipulated and controlled. Nahum 3:4 ESV states, *"And all for the countless whorings of the prostitute, graceful and of deadly charms, who betrays nations with her whorings, and peoples with her charms."* Sexuality and magic go hand in hand with many people who practice sorcery and witchcraft. Queen Jezebel used both tactics in her time as queen of Israel. Like the witch kings of the J.R.R Tolkien's *Lord of the Rings* books, Jezebel was a witch queen.

Jezebel being viewed as a practitioner of magic is seen in 2 Kings 9:22 ESV which states, *"And when Joram saw Jehu, he said, "Is it peace Jehu?" He answered, "What peace can there be, so long as the whorings and the sorceries of your mother Jezebel are so many?"*

Jezebel came from the bloodline of a priest of the goddess Astarte, her father Ithobaal I. Her brother was a king named Baal-Eser II. The mother of Jezebel is not known. However, there is a way to at least speculate as to what kind of woman she would have been based on the practices of the priests of Astarte such as her father Ithobaal I.

The way to identify what kind of woman the mother of Jezebel was is to look at the religious and royal practices of the Phoenicians. The territories of the Phoenicians spread from Lebanon all the way to Spain. A place called Catalonia in Spain and her surrounding areas have yielded some very interesting Phoenician cultural sites. Among the surrounding areas of Catalonia that the Phoenicians controlled or had relations with were communities of wise women 'witches' that had held considerable power in their day.

It was very rare to come across a woman who held power in certain areas of ancient times. It was even more rare to come across groups of women who had 'feminist' ideals to empower them to positions of power within a man's world. Yet, the Phoenicians were among one of the few civilizations that had such women.

The Phoenicians had a trade empire that extended to areas in *Aragon* and *Catalonia*, Spain. Catalonia had ancient areas that are sacred to people that stretch all the way back to prehistoric times. Neanderthals had ceremonial caves in the area that would later be used for other reasons. Caves are important in the world of magic. There are underwater caves in the surrounding areas of Catalonia that were possibly sacred sites to many people of feminine religions in their times when they were accessible.

The towns in the areas around Catalonia had and keep female names to keep relationships to their ancient goddesses they revered such as the towns of *Verges* (virgins or priestesses), *Estartit* (Astarte), *Roses* (rose lineage), and other towns named for their sacred wells and fountains. Catalonia's root name, *Catalunya*, is derived from a Celtic lunar name that refers to the descent of the moon.

Jezebel had a family that was dedicated to Astarte and Baal. Her father and brothers names were proof of their dedication to the Hittite and Canaanite god Baal. Her father was the priest of Astarte or Asherah. Here is the next point of interest in regards to her mother and Jezebel.

While the mystical practices of the Phoenicians have been outlined in the previous paragraphs, there is one thing that has not yet been mentioned that is of great fascination. The Phoenicians were Canaanites. They called themselves Canaanites even when they were no longer in the land of Canaan after Israel, Judah, and other empires had conquered it. Such a revelation is important when studying the roots of Jezebel.

Deuteronomy 18:14 ESV states, *"For these nations, which you are about to dispossess, listen to fortune-tellers and to diviners. But as for you, the Lord your God has not allowed you to do this."* Witchcraft has attracted many people in today's age. The allure of magic is the same as the fascination with the supernatural. People who practice Wiccan and witchcraft believe that magic will have five things happen to them to better their lives. Those five things through magic are listed as:

1. **Answers that will come to them when they are relaxed, asking for them, meditating on them, or sleeping on them.**
2. **They will have synchronicity happen in their lives. Opportunities they didn't even know to look for will occur.**
3. **They will notice other people's mistakes before the people themselves see it happen. This is called premonition.**
4. **They won't ever stop being curious or asking questions.**
5. **They will start to see things that they can't explain that will change reality for them and their faith in reality.**

People who put their faith in magic think that they will perceive and receive a higher plane of existence in nature through magical practices. What they don't realize is that they are not fully grasping the fact that the elements they are inviting into their lives can and usually are extremely dangerous.

1 Samuel 15:23 ESV says, *"For rebellion is as the sin of divination, and presumption is as iniquity and idolatry. Because you have rejected the word of the Lord, He has also rejected you from being king."* Magic is a form of rebellion. It is represented as a category in the study of religion and social sciences to define multiple practices and ideas considered separate to science and religion. Magic is a form of paranormal activity in its rawest form. Although seen as practice of using nature that can be controlled through such things as spells and incantations, the truth is far different than what is actually believed.

Magic is a way for people to "believe" they are controlling the world around them by their own power. In actuality, people who believe in magic or that they can control it are living a lie. The difference is that the people who are practicing magic don't know they are living a lie. Yes, there are people who know magic is not real or able to be controlled. And yes, there are people who believe it's real and can be controlled. Those people are duped into thinking that they have the power to control magic. They believe that the illusion is real. The ironic thing is that when some of the things magic practitioners see turn out to be real are things people wish were fake.

Magic comes from the Persian word *magu*. Magu is applied to a form of religious functionary about which very little is known. Originally varied between positive and negative uses, magic was later categorized as a negative element that was seen as being associated with demons, enchantments, divination, and other practices of the occult. The rise of humanism would reshape the viewpoint of magic.

Humanists in the early days of "modern Europe" reinterpreted magic in a positive sense with establishing it as having a part in natural forces and thus called it "natural magic." [12]

Magic was practiced in the religions of Canaan. Canaanite magic was performed in three types of magic. The types of magic Canaanites used were "divine magic" for reaching the gods, "folk magic" for common people to use, and then witchcraft and sorcery that would best be described as "black magic." Priests of temples would practice divine magic that encompassed divination, oracles, prophesies, healing, and astrology. Folk magic incorporated amulets and talismans for warding off evil spirits, curses, knots, dolls (like voodoo dolls but not called voodoo dolls), necromancy, serpent charming, and so on. Cursing was seen as evil, but was acceptable in common peoples magic as even the "gods" were prone to cursing people.

Necromancy was the one magic practice that was very taboo. Only at certain times was the act of summoning the dead or coming into contact with ghosts allowed, and only under very extreme conditions and situations. To the Canaanites, coming into contact with ghosts made someone impure and unclean. This practice is slightly similar to the Jewish belief of not touching a dead body following death, and would thus make someone ritually unclean if committed.

Witches and sorcerers are not viewed positively in Canaanite religion. In ancient Canaanite temples there existed exorcists that were on hand to combat against evil spells of witches. Witches, according to the Canaanites, were people who used black magic, consorted with demons, and

---

[12] Humanism- A philosophical and ethical stance that emphasizes the value and agency of human beings, individually and collectively, and generally prefers critical thinking and evidence over acceptance of dogma or superstition.

used spells that are harmful to others. The people of Canaanite temples who practiced magic were people that were viewed as healers and breakers of curses. Those who would use magic to harm others were seen as dangerous and wicked.

To the ancient peoples of Canaan, things such as divination, healing, exorcism, prayer, and astrology were not viewed as evil practices of magic. Those types of practices were seen as ways to reach the divine or the gods. In short, divine magic was used to reach the gods, folk magic for local customs and superstitions, and witchcraft for black magic and evil. To use witchcraft in the eyes of the Canaanites was impious, and its practice was an act of evil before the gods.

In Babylon, witches could be executed for casting spells on other people. In Canaan, witches were not viewed as good but were allowed to live. The Semitic names for witches and sorcerers were the *Chaberim* and *Kashapim*. The Kashapim were sorcerers who cast spells to harm others. Sorcerers were viewed differently than witches as they were sometimes seen as healers that used magic and herbs for "good." However, most were seen as a negative influence, and therefore harmful and dangerous like witches.

Sorcerers had a standing in Canaanite temples. While not temple priests, they did appear sometimes in royal courts similar to how magicians were present among the royal courts of Egypt. Canaanite society viewed witches and sorcerers as evil and didn't usually allow them within cities and towns. To find a witch in Canaan, the most common place was outside of cities among the local tribes.

Several tribes had witches or sorcerers who performed magical acts. Women were the main source of witches, though there were some men. The name for a male witch is warlock, but the word witch has been applied interchangeably to men and women equally. In the southern deserts of Canaan, the wandering Arab tribes such as the Nabataeans had female witches who would tell fortunes for money. In cities among the more educated, witches who told fortunes were viewed mostly as charlatans that used tricks to gain money from the uneducated and stupid people who fell for the cons of the witches. Today, there are people who will buy goods from "magic shops" simply because they believe that if they don't the people selling them will curse them with black magic or some other form of dark magic.

Magic isn't real, but there are people who believe it is legitimate. The ancient world makes proof of that. When the Hebrews arrived on the scene in Canaan, they viewed magic as evil no matter who practiced it. Among the Hebrews, sorcerers and witches were to be sentenced to death. Moses and Aaron had to battle against magic users in Egypt when they were freeing the Hebrews from 430 years of slavery and bondage. It took ten plagues including the death of every first born in Egypt to break the Pharaoh and free the people of Israel. God didn't want the practices of the Egyptians or the Canaanites to influence His people, as He knew that while "magic" was fake, there were real spiritual forces that worked behind the scenes with magic.

The Hebrews and Canaanites shared a similar view on mediums and necromancers. Leviticus 19:31 ESV states, *"Do not turn to mediums or necromancers; do not seek them out, and so make yourselves unclean by them: I am the Lord your God."* The Hebrews viewed those that interacted with ghosts and spirits as unclean similar to how the Canaanites viewed such acts. The main reason God forbid such practices was because of the influence a spirit could have over someone that was listening to a person who channeled a spirit or called upon someone from death.

Deuteronomy 18:9-12 ESV reads:

"When you come into the land that the Lord your God is giving you, you shall not learn to follow the abominable practices of these nations. There shall not be found among you anyone who burns his son or his daughter as an offering, anyone who practices divination or tells fortunes or interprets omens, or a sorcerer or a charmer or a medium or a necromancer or one who inquires of the dead, for whoever does these things is an abomination to the Lord. And because of these abominations the Lord your God is driving them out before you."

Notice the difference between a necromancer and one who inquires of the dead in the scripture. As mentioned, there is always a difference in practices and beliefs that, while similar or identical, are two vastly different things. God understood this and instructed the Jewish people on such differences so they wouldn't be caught unaware.

Judges 5:8 ESV says, *"When new gods were chosen, then war was in the gates. Was shield or spear to be seen among forty thousand in Israel?"* Two conflicting ideologies, practices, or gods will always bring war. The most effective type of warfare is psychological warfare. Warring on the mind can bring uncertainty. When a king, queen, or leader has an uncertain mind, then they will be open to anything. They can become controlled by something that wants to possess them for whatever purposes the possessor wishes. King Saul in the Bible was one such ruler that allowed an enemy to take hold in his mind.

King Saul was unstable in his mind for most of his life following a decision by God to remove him as king and give the crown of Israel over to King David. Saul possibly suffered from what is known as dysphoric mania. The psychological definition of dysphoric mania is a mixed mania or mixing of symptoms. It refers to a group of symptoms that features into bipolar disorder. About fifty percent of those that suffer from bipolar disorder experience dysphoric mania. Those that are dysphoric are seen as one who is unhappy, full of anxiety, and similar to being depressed. It is the opposite of euphoric where the feelings are often positive and happy. People that are dysphoric are constantly feeling negative about life.

King Saul had lost his relationship with God and the Holy Spirit. During one very brutal war that he was in, Saul was desperate to seek guidance. There were two prophets that were in Israel during Saul's reign. The prophet Nathan was not present during the war, and the Nazarite prophet and judge Samuel had recently died. Saul had a special connection with Samuel, as he was the one who anointed Saul king, and who also removed the crown from Saul at the command of God and placed it and the anointing of kingship on the shoulders of David. Though dead, Saul sought the council of one who spoke to God such as Samuel. With Nathan gone, Saul decided to seek out a witch to call upon the spirit of Samuel.

One night Saul found such a witch. The witch of Endor was a medium that could "allegedly" raise up the dead from the earth. Saul came to her in secret and told her that he wished to speak to the spirit of Samuel. 1 Samuel 28:7 ESV states, *"Then Saul said to his servants, "Seek out for me a woman who is a medium, that I may go to her and inquire of her." And his servants said to him, "Behold, there is a medium at En-dor."* The KJV reading of the scripture describes the woman as having a familiar spirit.

A familiar spirit is identified as a demon or evil spirit that is said to attend and obey a witch. It is believed that a familiar spirit often takes the form of an animal. The term familiar is a term from the Latin word *familiaris* meaning "house servant." The thing that most people never realize is that a familiar spirit is not under the control of the witch. Rather, the witch is under the control of the familiar spirit.

2 Thessalonians 2:2 ESV reads, *"Not to be quickly shaken in mind or alarmed, either by a spirit or a spoken word, or a letter seeming to be from us, to the effect that the day of the Lord has come."* People shouldn't be afraid of what a spirit might say. A person should be mindful of what they hear, but when someone claims to hear something from a 'spirit' they need to make sure it is legitimate as chances are its nothing more than lies. 1 John ESV says, *"Beloved, do not believe every spirit, but test the spirits to see whether they are from God, for many false prophets have gone out into the world."* Further, 1 Timothy 4:1 states, *"Now the Spirit expressly says that in later times some will depart from the faith by devoting themselves to deceitful spirits and teachings of demons."*

Witches are not always driven into witchcraft because they are seeking some "new thing" in life to see if it is trendy and cool. A lot of people embrace witchcraft because they are shunned and oppressed. People join cults and new age movements to be accepted usually because they are seeking an environment that is safe and secure. They long to be accepted, find their place in life, and to attain power to better their position in the world. This should be the church. It should be a safe and secure place where one can find Jesus and the Holy Spirit.

Zephaniah 1:4-5 NAS says, *"So I will stretch out My hand against Judah and against all the inhabitants of Jerusalem. And I will cut off the remnant of Baal from this place, and the names of the idolatrous priests along with the priests."* Two sets of priests are named in the scriptures. One set is the idolatrous priests, and the other set is the regular priests. Idolatrous is defined as worshiping idols or treating someone or something as an idol. Idols are cult images that can be seen in the form of a physical image such as an icon or a statue. The reason for the mention of the differences in priests from Zephaniah 1:4-5 is to show that as there is a difference in priests, there is also a difference in the witches of the Bible.

According to the historian Josephus, the witch of Endor was not a witch at all. She was in his opinion a sorceress or necromancer. However, necromancy is used in witchcraft. Whether or not Josephus was correct is still debatable. It is more likely the witch of Endor was an actual witch due to her association with a medium spirit, her summoning of the dead, and her practices resembling those of the Canaanite witches. The area of Endor is interesting as it is possibly located in the Jezreel Valley's southern edge in Israel. The area would be in what is known as Tell Qedesh, or Tell el-Ajyul/El-Ajyul where a cave with a spring in it is located. The significance of a cave with a spring likely is where the witch kept what is known as an *Ob* or ritual pit for summoning the dead.

Jezebel has a connection to the witch of Endor by way of the use of witchcraft with the use of an ob. There is an interesting description of the ritual practices of Ahab after he married Jezebel. 1 Kings 16:32-34 ESV states, *"He erected an altar for Baal in the house of Baal, which he built in Samaria. And Ahab made an Asherah. Ahab did more to provoke the Lord, the God of Israel, to anger than all the kings of Israel who were before him. In his days Hiel of Bethel built Jericho. He laid its foundations at the cost of Abiram his firstborn, and set up its gates at the cost of his youngest son Segub, according to the word of the Lord, which he spoke by Joshua the son of Nun."*

Notice the use of the "cost" of the sons of Hiel. It is likely that these children were sacrificed in ceremonies to appease the gods of Jezebel and Ahab. Jezebel possibly had Ahab rebuild Jericho for the purpose of conducting ritual sacrifice for her worship of other Phoenicians gods aside from Baal. The others gods in this case would be goddesses.

Jezebel's people of Sidon had a special reverence for female deities. Remembering the scripture that describes women as the glory of men brings to mind the seen but often not pointed out reverence civilizations have for women.

162

Witches, whether male or female, paid special attention to the attraction of feminine qualities brought through witchcraft.

The spiritual nature of witchcraft is of a negative feminine nature. Both feminine and masculine can be symbols of positive empowerment that people can grow and thrive under if it is done in the correct way. Negative feminine spirits can produce a spirit of addiction. There is only one scripture in the Bible that uses the word addiction, at least in the English rendering of the word. However, the meaning of the word "addiction" that is found in 1 Corinthians 16:15 is appropriate.

1 Corinthians 16:15-16 KJV states:

"I beseech you brethren, (ye know the house of Stephanas, that it is the first fruits of Achaia, and that they have addicted themselves to serving saints, I urge you that ye submit yourselves unto such, and to everyone that helpeth with us, and laboureth."

While a scripture about being addicted to the service of God, there is another point to be made when the scripture is observed. Carefully manipulated, addiction can be molded into a form of servitude, or even into a form of slavery.

Addiction can make anyone into a slave. It can turn even the strongest of individuals into the lowliest of creatures. It takes a long time to get over an addiction in certain situations such as drug and alcohol addiction. God can remove the curse of addiction from people, but a person must always remember to keep themselves above the allure of the things that can bring about addiction. This is where faith is a powerful weapon for if faith can move mountains, then it can surely remove the burden of addiction from a person's shoulders. God gave mankind faith to resist temptation and

Map of Jericho With Labyrinth Style Walls. A Labyrinth is a Symbol Used in Magic. Courtesy of Humus Sapiens.

addiction just as Jesus resisted narcotics when he died on the cross. Jesus would not allow anything to replace His faith. God expects mankind to use faith the same way.

The ways that addiction is manifested in its purest raw forms are listed in Galatians 5:19-21 ESV that says, *"Now the works of the flesh are evident: sexual immorality, impurity, sensuality, idolatry, sorcery, enmity, strife, jealousy, fits of anger, rivalries, dissensions, divisions, envy, drunkenness, orgies, and things like these. I warn you as I warned you before, that those who do such things will not inherit the kingdom of God."*

The King James Bible and the New International Bible replace the word sorcery with the word witchcraft. Addiction is a key element in witchcraft. It provides the followers of such ways with a belief of control and power either as the controller or the controlled.

Ahab was addicted to Jezebel. He clung to her like a prostitute stays with an abusive pimp. Everything that he did in the name of her gods was all for what Jezebel wanted. She hated the God of Abraham, Isaac, and Israel (Jacob). She used her sex, beauty, influence, and words to wrap Ahab around her fingers. Her influence was made through the word of the king. The rebuilding of Jericho during her reign as queen was likely used as a way to make a city of witchcraft. Jericho has been the site of several interesting finds in archaeology. Among them were what is known as *Teraphim* or plastered skulls that were used for divination and ancestor worship. Maps of Jericho with the walls resembling a labyrinth have been unearthed as well.

Labyrinths are a type of symbol used in magic for control of a spiritual center, a nature, and are used to create traps for demons and other creatures by placing them within the center of the maze as a labyrinth is a maze by design. They are also used for the purpose of finding a person's inner center as people in a labyrinth are a reflection of the lost looking for answers, finding one's spiritual self, or seeking the need for inner peace. Pits have also been uncovered in or around Jericho where many of the plastered skulls were found. It is possible these pits were obs for summoning the dead, or ritual sacrifice pits for the purpose of religion, sorcery, or witchcraft. It needs to be noted that the actual use of the pits could be one or all three, but is still largely unknown.

The goddess of witchcraft in ancient Greece is known as

Hecate. She is often depicted as a goddess with triple heads, carrying twin torches, and is associated with both life and death. Her familiars, like most witches possess, were dogs. While at times witches have cats or birds like crows or ravens as their familiars, Hecate has dogs as her familiars. Dogs were sacrificed to Hecate at crossroads, such as those found in modern highways and roadways, as crossroads were viewed as areas that deals were made with demons or spirits. What is an interesting connection between Hecate, dogs, witchcraft, and Jezebel in the Bible is the way that Jezebel died at the end of her reign as queen of Israel.

Jezebel met her death at the hands of some eunuchs who tossed her out an open window when a man named Jehu came and ordered her execution. While Jehu called her a cursed woman, he recognized her as a king's daughter and ordered her to be buried like royalty out of respect for her position as queen. But, in 2 Kings 9:35, when they went to bury her there was nothing left but her skull, feet, and the palms of her hands. The dogs of the Jezreel territory had eaten Jezebel. This was prophetic as God told the prophet Elijah in 2 Kings 9:36-37 ESV which reads, *"This is the word of the Lord, which He spoke by his servant Elijah the Tishbite: 'In the territory of Jezreel the dogs shall eat the flesh of Jezebel, and the corpse of Jezebel shall be as dung on the face of the field in the territory of Jezreel, so that no one can say, this is Jezebel."*

God put an end to the witch queen Jezebel in Jezreel which was the same territory that the witch of Endor was believed to have resided. He ended her life by throwing her from a high place, and erased her identity. Her erasing was in reference to "no one can say this is Jezebel." Using dogs, which were the symbol of a witch goddess, seemed like a perfect poetic justice to erase Jezebel from existence. Just like Lucifer was thrown down so was Jezebel thrown down to death.

The use of the female spirit in league with witchcraft is due to the huge attraction it brings both physically and spiritually to those influenced by witchcraft. The duality of the image of witchcraft favors the female form more than a male as a woman is seen as far more spiritual than men when it comes to the natural world, purity, and beauty. The image of Venus is a major influence in the ancient world and in modern times. Many modern feminist movements use the symbol of Venus in their political and social organizations. The image of Venus is celestial, astrological, astronomical, and religious in origin. A particular group of people in the ancient world possibly was the originators of the image of Venus through their association with star worship. Those people are whom the Bible refers to as the *Nephilim*.

The Nephilim were the giant and mighty offspring of angels and humans who had sexual relations with one another. While the Bible makes mention mainly of men as Nephilim, there are some passages that mention female Nephilim. There is evidence of some of the mothers of the male Nephilim that could in fact be female angels. In the next chapter will be evidence of the daughters of God and the sons of men with their connection to the possible rise of magic, gods and goddesses. There will also be theories as to the images that mankind associated with the planets and stars of the heavens.

CHAPTER 12: DAUGHTERS OF GOD & MIGHTY WOMEN

Genesis 6:4 ESV says, *"The Nephilim were on the earth in those days, and also afterward, when the sons of God came into the daughters of man and they bore children to them. These were the mighty men of old, the men of renown."* This scripture in the beginning of Genesis six is one of the most examined and studied Bible verses in the world. It has been enlightening, controversial, and educational to those that devoted themselves to the study of the Nephilim. There is an old saying that a single scripture in the Bible can lead to a lifetime of study. Genesis 6:4 is one such scripture that can span a person's entire existence.

The term "sons of God" is in reference to angels. With the application of the word 'sons' brings the identification of the angels as male figures. However, if the sons of God were having sex with human women and producing offspring, then there comes to mind a completely new question? Were there daughters of God who had sexual relations with the sons of man? More so, did those daughters of God have husbands?

The reference to angels and humans marrying comes from Genesis 6:2 ESV, which states, *"The sons of God saw that the daughters of man were attractive. And they took as their wives any that they chose."* Here is the wording and identification of angels and humans taking matrimonial positions with each other. While a topic of debate, this scripture at the least provides evidence for another old saying "Where in scripture can you find that?" Backing up topics with scripture is important and imperative. The hard part is where to look for proof in the Bible.

It is vital to study and work the Bible through every translation, word, and detail for even the slightest bit of information. Such study and devotion will help with the research, proofing, and reproofing of the mysteries that the

Bible holds. One of Clint Eastwood's best lines from his movie *A Fistful of Dollars* is "In these parts, even a spec of information can be worth its weight in gold." Every small piece of information and detail can go a long way in the Word of God.

The Bible does mention names of female angels. There is mention of the names of some of the possible sons of those angels. Also, there is made mention of two possible daughters of those angels. Yes, women giants are mentioned in the Bible and they are unique in their identities. The first thing to examine though is the daughters of God, their names, and their possible offspring.

Isaiah 29:1-7 ESV reads:

"Ah, Ariel, Ariel, the city where David encamped! Add year to year; let the feasts run their round. Yet I will distress Ariel, and there shall be moaning and lamentation, and she shall be to me like an Ariel. And I will encamp against you all around, and will besiege you with towers and I will raise siege works against you. And you be brought low; from the earth you shall speak, and from the dust your speech will be bowed down; your voice shall come from the ground like the voice of a ghost, and from the dust your speech shall whisper. But the multitude of your foreign foes shall be like small dust, and the multitude of the ruthless like passing chaff. And in an instant suddenly, you will be visited by the Lord of hosts with thunder and with earthquake and great noise, with the whirlwind and tempest, and the flame of a devouring fire. And the multitude of all the nations that fight against Ariel, all that fight against her and her stronghold and distress her, shall be like a dream, a vision of the night."

Ariel translates into "lion of God" and "hearth of God." The name Ariel is identified in the Bible as representing three things. The city of Jerusalem is referred to as Ariel. A town itself in Israel is named Ariel. Then, there is a female angel named Ariel. The place mentioned in Isaiah 29:1-7 is not the

Handle of the Gebel-el-Arak Knife of Egypt. Image Depicts Levantine Man or God Handling two Lions as the Master of Animals. Courtesy of Calimenronte.

City of Jerusalem. It doesn't necessarily refer either to the town of Ariel. The scripture possibly refers to the country of Moab.

2 Samuel 23:20 ESV states, *"And Benaiah the son of Jehoiada was a valiant man of Kabzeel, a doer of great deeds. He struck down two Ariels of Moab. He also went down and struck down a lion in a pit on a day when snow had fallen."* In the KJV translation, the 'Ariels of Moab' is interpreted as two "lion like" men. Other

translations have called the two lion like men "sons of Ariel." Interesting identification when one observes the people of Moab in closer study.

Lion is translated from the compounding of two Hebrew words: *ariy* and *el.* Ariy means 'lion' or 'image of a lion,' and 'el' means god, angel, or even demon in some definitions of the word. The use of Ariel to describe the Moab warriors should not be confused with descriptions of lions with other people such as the Gadites that fought for King David in 1 Chronicles 12:8 ESV:

"From the Gadites there went over to David at the stronghold in the wilderness mighty and experienced warriors, experts with shield and spear, whose faces were like the faces of lions and who were swift as gazelles upon the mountains..."

The Gadites were described as men with faces like lions while the warriors of Moab were simply called Ariels.

Another interesting description from biblical scripture that makes the Moabites unique among other warriors is found in 1 Chronicles 11:22 ESV:

"And Benaiah the son of Jehoiada was a valiant man of Kabzeel, a doer of great deeds. He struck down two heroes of Moab. He also went down and struck down a lion in a pit when the snow had fallen."

The term hero is applied to the two Ariels in the 1 Chronicles 11:22 scripture. Heroes was a title associated with the Nephilim of Genesis 6:4. The connection between the Ariels of Moab and the Nephilim can be made through the possible mother of the 'sons of Ariel.'

There is much debate about who Ariel was in the Bible. Early researchers of the *Book of Enoch* have claimed that the name Ariel is mentioned, but some modern scholars have

172

attested that the name Ariel is not mentioned through recent translation and examination. While debatable, the possible mention of Ariel in the Book of Enoch and other mentions associated with the name Ariel have led to the belief that Ariel is an angel. It is very likely Ariel is a fallen angel.

Ariel is possibly one of the angels who came to the earth with the Watchers. The Watchers were a group of angels who took human wives and taught them lessons in warfare, astronomy and astrology, and magic. While debatable, the mention of the sons of Ariel from the land of Moab can be connected to another woman in the Bible of non-angelic origins. This alleged woman and mother of giants also came from Moab. That woman is the sister of Ruth (who King David descends from) and the mother of Goliath and his brothers known as Orpah.

Orpah and Ruth were Moabites who married Israelites that died and left them childless. Ruth and her mother in law Naomi left Moab for Judah, but Orpah stayed behind as Ruth 1:14 ESV states, *"Then they lifted up their voices and wept again. And Orpah kissed her mother-in-law, but Ruth clung to her."* Naomi didn't want her daughter-in-laws to go with her to Judah. While Ruth convinced Naomi to take her to Judah, Orpah stayed behind. The kiss Orpah gave Naomi was a kiss good-bye as they parted ways for the rest of their lives.

Orpah was believed to have been the mother of the Philistine giants Goliath, Ishbi-Benob, Saph, Sippai, and Lahmi. Goliath and his brothers were considered champions of the Philistines. Heroes and champions went hand in hand in ancient Greece and the Levant, as heroes became champions through contests of strength and war. Being a Moabite woman, Orpah gives credibility to the possibility that the people of Moab had descended from the Nephilim. With that connection then comes a plausible argument that Ariel may have been a matriarch of the Moabite nation. The

173

nation of the Moabites came from incest between Lot, the nephew of Abraham, and Lot's daughters. However, the children of Lot obviously married other people from other tribes and people that would thus create the civilization and nation of Moab through growth from generation to generation.

The Moabites shared similar to same religions as the Phoenicians by way of child sacrificing. One of the kings of Moab mentioned in 2 Kings 3:4 was named Mesha. He was a sheep breeder who had to deliver over 100,000 lambs and wool of rams as tribute to the king of Israel. Mesha later rebelled against Israel in a losing effort. During the final part of the campaign Israel waged against Moab, King Mesha made a sacrifice of his son to a fire. 2 Kings 3:27 ESV states, *"Then he took his oldest son who was to reign in his place and offered him for a burnt offering on the wall. And there came great wrath against Israel. And they withdrew from him and returned to their own land."* The Moabites, Phoenicians, and Babylonians practiced child sacrifice.

Why did Israel withdraw from the campaign against the Moabites after seeing such a sacrifice? It is likely not because the Israelites were afraid of some divine intervention by a Moabite god as the Israelites had Yahweh on there side. Rather, it could be that the sacrifice (allegedly) showed that the Moabites were willing to sacrifice themselves or commit Kamikaze (suicide attacks) against the Israelite army as it most likely was about to become a Moabite last stand.

Rather than fight against the sons of Ariel in a battle that possibly would have cost countless Israelite lives, the people of Israel simply withdrew from the battle. There was no need to risk the possibility of senseless killings of many against an already defeated people as the Moabites lost most if not all of their cities, territories, and wealth against the Israelites up to the point of the sacrifice by King Mesha.

The sacrifice of King Mesha's son was made to the Moabite god Chemosh. The kingdom of Ebla located in Syria worshiped the same god but pronounced Chemosh as Kamish. Chemosh was also the deity worshiped by the Amorites.

The Amorites were another Semitic tribe from Ur like the Israelites according to Judges 11:23-24 ESV which reads, *"So then the Lord, the God of Israel, dispossessed the Amorites from before His people Israel; and are you to take possession of them? Will you not possess what Chemosh your god gives you to possess? And all that the Lord our God has dispossessed before us, we will possess."*

It is alleged that Chemosh was also worshiped by the Ammonites, the cousin nation to the Moabites. Chemosh was associated with the Semitic mother- goddess Ashtar. She is often called Ashtar-Chemosh. She is further identical to Astarte aka Asherah. The name Chemosh-Ashtar was to create a more masculine pronunciation, which was used throughout Southern Arabia. The name is further seen in other wording by way of the reversing of the name in Ashtar-Chemosh. This was likely to create a stronger pushing of the goddess for worship on the same level as the god Baal as Chemosh-Ashtar was viewed on the same level of authority.

Israel was introduced to Chemosh at Mount Pe'or. The prophet Balaam made a sacrifice to God on the mountaintop to God and blessed Israel. The Israelites in contrast to Balaam later became involved with Moabite women and culture, which developed an interest in Moabite gods. They joined a cult dedicated to the worship of Baal Pe'or (the use of the name Pe'or in front of Baal is due to the location of the cult on Mount Pe'or).

A reference to the incident is made mention in Revelation 2:14 ESV which says, *"But I have a few things against you: you have some there who hold the teaching of Balaam, who taught Balak to put a stumbling block before the sons of Israel, so that they might eat food sacrificed to idols and practice sexual immorality."*

Israel was involved with Baal Pe'or on Mount Pe'or in the same way that King Solomon involved himself and Israel with the worship of Chemosh-Ashtar.[13]

King Solomon set up temples to Chemosh through the wives he had taken. Many of them most likely came from Moab. 1 Kings 11:7 ESV states, *"Then Solomon built a high place for Chemosh the abomination of Moab, and for Molech the abomination of the Ammonites, on the mountain east of Jerusalem.*

King Josiah would later destroy the temples dedicated to Chemosh in 2 Kings 23:13 ESV that reads, *"And the king defiled the high places that were east of Jerusalem, to the south of the mount of corruption, which Solomon the king of Israel had built for Ashtoreth the abomination of the Sidonians, and for Chemosh the abomination of Moab, and for Milcom the abomination of the Ammonites."*

Solomon had allowed himself to become influenced by his wives to abandon Yahweh in exchange for child sacrificing gods and religions. He had forgotten the gifts of God that gave him wisdom, wealth, power, and a great name among the nations. Solomon had allowed his power to corrupt him. As the old saying goes, "Power corrupts, and absolute power corrupts absolutely!"

---

[13] Baal Pe'or is not known to be associated with any other incarnations of Baal. It is believed Baal Pe'or is associated with or is Chemosh due to Baal Pe'or being a Moabite god and the cult originating from Moab. Baal in this case is being used in a licentious manner meaning used without accepted rules of his actual identity, and instead for personal purposes of the cult most likely to lure people in for sexual conduct.

*Simple Seal of Solomon (Top) and a Moroccan 1873 AD Falus Coin
with the Seal of Solomon. Courtesy of Securiger, Pitoutom, and Jpb
1301.

King Solomon had a hand in the creation of many symbols that are used in magic and witchcraft. A symbol called the *Seal of Solomon* was the signet ring attributed to Solomon that would later become the inspiration for the Star of David. The seal is depicted in several forms including a pentagram and hexagram shape. The legend behind the Seal of Solomon is that the ring signet gave Solomon the power to command demons, jinn (also known as genies), and the ability to speak to animals. Along with the fame of the wisdom of Solomon, the ring's symbolism became famous for being made into talismans, amulets, and later used in medieval and Renaissance-era magic, occult, and alchemy practices.

The stories of the Seal of Solomon came predominately from Medieval Arabic writers who saw the seal as a blessing from God given directly to Solomon from Heaven. An interesting connection can be made between Solomon, his seal, and Arabs by way of the queen of Sheba. Known as Bilquis in Arabic and the name Makeda in Ethiopian, the Queen of Sheba came from the country of Sheba believed to be located in Southern Arabia in what is modern day Yemen.

Makeda and Solomon met after she was intrigued by his wisdom. 1 Kings 10:1 ESV says, *"Now when the queen of Sheba heard of Solomon concerning the name of the Lord, she came to test him with hard questions."* After her inquiries, Makeda was quite impressed with Solomon and the wisdom he possessed. She gave praise to God, and was impressed with what Solomon had done with his kingdom. 1 Kings 10:13 ESV states, *"And King Solomon gave to the queen of Sheba all that she desired, whatever she asked besides what was given to her by the bounty of King Solomon. So she turned and went back to her own land with her servants."* It is believed that Solomon and Makeda were lovers.

There are stories that the queen of Sheba gave birth to a royal lineage that helped established the modern nation of Ethiopia. The wording in 1 Kings 10:13 in league with the scripture reading of Ecclesiastes 7:28 in chapter nine gives rise to the possibility that Solomon was very much devoted to Bilquis. It is likely he was madly in love and totally obsessed with her. Makeda is considered to be a very beautiful woman. Power and beauty were just some of the things that made the queen of Sheba one of the most famous women in history. Another part to her history that if true, makes Bilquis very unique among women.

It is speculated that the queen of Sheba was part Jinn. Jinn were considered to be the Rephaim or giants who descended from the Nephilim. Another belief is that Jinn are the Shedim of Psalm 106:37 and Deuteronomy 32:17. The Shedim are demons or spirits that sons and daughters were sacrificed to in Canaan.

Verses in Psalm 106:36-38 gives account of what happens when people sacrificed to the Shedim. Psalm 106:36-38 ESV states, *"They served their idols, which became a snare to them. They sacrificed their sons and their daughters to the demons; they poured out innocent blood, the blood of their sons and daughters, whom they sacrificed to the idols of Canaan, and the land was polluted with blood."*

Further reading in Deuteronomy 32:16-17 ESV gives more testimony to the results of sacrificing to the Shedim:

"They stirred Him to jealously with strange gods; with abominations they provoked Him to anger. They sacrificed to demons that were no gods, to gods they had never known, to new gods that had come recently, whom your fathers had never dreaded."

Human sacrifices were offered to Shedim (demons) and Chadashim (new gods) that were an affront to God. Interesting of note, the mother of the Shedim is the demon Lilith in Jewish legend. Lilith is also the mother of another demonic class called the Lilim. Lilim are daughters of Lilith instead of sons.

179

Like the Shedim, the Rephaim are considered by many modern scholars to be demons. More specifically, they are considered to be where evil spirits or demons came from after a giant or giants had died. Though only speculation, the Bible does mention a possible connection to the Rephaim as either evil spirits or dead ancestors in Isaiah 14:9, Isaiah 26:14, Proverbs 2:18, Proverbs 9:18, Proverbs 21:16, and Job 26:5. Aside from the demonic references, the Rephaim are mentioned among a multitude of giants that were wiped out in a war in Genesis 14:5-6 ESV:

"In the fourteenth year Chedorlaomer and the kings who were with him came and defeated the Rephaim in Ashteroth-karnaim, the Zuzim in Ham, the Emim in Shaveh-kiriathaim, and the Horites in their hill country of Seir as far as El-paran on the border of the wilderness."

It is not truly known if the queen of Sheba is a Rephaim. But, the kingdom of Sheba and the country of Yemen have remains of an alleged giant civilization that built an ancient world marvel called the Marib Dam in 750 B.C. that lasted for over 1,000 years, until finally bursting in 600 A.D. The people who built the Marib Dam and lived in Sheba are known as the Sabaeans. While not necessarily Sabaeans, there are those in the world who do claim to have some ancestry from supernatural beings in the modern world such as the Mahra tribe of Yemen who claim some ancestry to Jinn.[14]

King Solomon possibly created the Seal of Solomon through interactions with the Sabaeans. The Sabaeans had several kingdoms spread throughout Yemen and Ethiopia. There are temples that housed particular geometric shapes, characteristic and distinguishing colors, and were dedicated to

---

[14] Further study of the Nephilim can be found in the books *Age of Mystery* and *Investigating Wonders.*

the seven planets which in the ancient world was made up of the Moon, Mercury, Venus, the Sun, Mars, Jupiter, and Saturn. The Sabaeans had two sects to their religious practices. Those sects were those who worshiped stars and those who worshiped idols.

The seven planets were associated with seven gods or godships. Venus, of course, was associated with the goddess Ishtar. The Seal of Solomon is attributed to the seven planets. The seal is most likely a tribute to Makeda as the seal has similar designs to the Sabaean language, shares particular themes with the seven planets, and when used for talismans and magic will be written with angels, psalms, and ideas of love, protection, and cursing. It is only speculation, but it is likely that after Makeda left for Sheba that Solomon had lost his heart. Solomon was not satisfied with his 1000 wives or concubines, foreign gods, or even the blessings that God gave him. As he got older, Solomon possibly may have never gotten over Makeda. He possibly wrote the Song of Solomon for his unrequited love and desire.

Another man mentioned in the Bible possibly fell in love with a female Nephilim. That man is the father of Nimrod. Nimrods father was named Cush. Genesis 10:7-8 ESV reads, *"The sons of Cush: Seba, Havilah, Sabtah, Raamah, and Sabteca. The sons of Raamah: Sheba and Dedan. Cush fathered Nimrod; he was the first on earth to be a mighty man."* Nimrod is mentioned separate from the line of his brothers. The reason for this is due to the possibility that Cush had Nimrod either outside of marriage and likely because of who the mother of Nimrod is in history. He is certainly singled out among his brothers.

Nimrod's mother is a woman named Semiramis. Semiramis is an interesting figure as she is considered both mother and wife to Nimrod. She is the mother of a deity called Tammuz who is both son and brother to Nimrod. Tammuz is mentioned in Ezekiel 8:14 ESV:

181

"Then he brought me to the entrance of the north gate of the house of the Lord, and behold, there sat women weeping for Tammuz."

Tammuz is believed to be a possible king known as Dumuzid. Tammuz is the corrupted spelling of the name Dumuzid. He is listed as an antediluvian (pre-flood of Noah) king who was one of the earliest rulers of Uruk. Semiramis is considered to be an actual person from Mesopotamia and said to be the creator of polytheism and goddess worship. While many scholars have rejected the idea of Semiramis being the sole creator of polytheism and goddess worship, there are strong arguments that can be made which state she at least played a good part in their development. Much of the Babylonian religious practices are linked to her.

The Assyrian queen Shammuramat is attributed to Semiramis, but it is unlikely that these two women are one and the same due to the timelines in which they lived. Semiramis is considered to have been a queen of Assyria after marrying a king named Ninus. She restored Babylon after one of its points of destruction, built palaces in Persia, and conquered a portion of Asia at one point in time. She is considered a historical figure in Armenia, Assyria, and is considered sacred in Iraq, Syria, Turkey, and Iran (many girls are named after Semiramis).

Semiramis is said to be a possessive, lustful, and possessed the traits of a harlot. One Armenian legend tells how she went to war just to possess a prince that refused to sleep with her. She is said to be the daughter of the fish goddess Atargatis who is connected to Ishtar. Both Semiramis and Ishtar share the same symbol of a dove.

Semiramis is said to have been a sorceress or a witch. From the same story of the Armenian prince she sought to sleep with comes the story of how she tried to raise him from the dead after he had been killed in battle. While there are

182

many versions of the story, the one that is most accepted is that after failing to bring him back to life, she dressed up one of her lovers as the prince and convinced everyone she did indeed bring him back to life.

Doves and fish are associated with Semiramis. Both forms are linked to Astarte and Atargatis. These women are associated with the queen of heaven that is mentioned in the book of Jeremiah. The queen of heaven is found in Jeremiah 7:18 ESV which states, *"The children gathered wood, the fathers kindled fire, and the women knead dough, to make cakes for the queen of heaven. And they pour out drink offerings to other gods, to provoke me to anger."*

The queen of heaven is again mentioned in Jeremiah 44:25 ESV which states, *"Thus says the Lord of hosts, the God of Israel: You and your wives have declared with your mouths, and have fulfilled it with your hands, saying, 'We will surely perform our vows that we have made, to make offerings to the queen of heaven and to pour out drink offerings to her.' Then confirm your vows and perform your vows!"*

The term 'queen of heaven' is a term that is used today among contemporary pagans to refer to 'the great goddess.' The term is also used among many Christian denominations to refer to Mary the mother of Jesus as the queen of heaven.

The term applies to another goddess, Anath. Anath is a Semitic and Canaanite deity who is also the name of the mother of the legendary Israelite hero Shamgar who slaughtered over 600 Philistines in one battle. She and Shamgar are mentioned in Judges 3:31 ESV which reads, *"After him was Shamgar the son of Anath, who killed six hundred of the Philistines with an oxgoad, and he also saved Israel.* Then, Judges 5:6 ESV says, *"In he days of Shamgar, son of Anath, in the days of Jael, the highways were abandoned, and travelelers kept to the byways."* Shamgar is considered a demi-god or Nephilim. He has no introduction, conclusion, or references in his length of reign as a judge of Israel. Shamgar, more possibly spelled Shammah is a judge from when it was the worst time in Israel with village life collapsing and roads being abandoned. Based on the end wording of Judges 3:31, which says, "and he also save Israel," then it could be considered that Shamgar simply was killing Philistines and the saving of Israel was a simple additional bonus. This is of course mere speculation, yet is supported by descent evidence as mentioned from the wording of the scripture.

The Jewish Encyclopedia considers Shamgar a foreign oppressor instead of an actual Israelite judge. It is believed that Shamgar is a Hittite as the name Shamgar is found among Assyrian references to Hittite names.[15] Anath is also a name of a Canaanite deity and therefore like the sons of Aerial, Shamgar is a 'son of Anath.'[16]

Asherah, Anath, and Astarte are considered the queen of heaven. All three of these deities are considered different but interchangeable at times. There is another alleged female angel that is possibly attributed with Venus like the queens of heaven. Her name is Haniel.

Haniel (spelled with either one *n* or two) is considered one of the seven archangels or chief angels of God. Haniel can also be spelled as Anael, Hanael, or Aniel. While not mentioned as an angel, the name Haniel is found in the Bible.

---

[15] "Son of Anath" is a miitary designation among some Canaanite warriors used as a sign of protection.

[16] Anath has two cities named after her in Ben-Anath in Lebanon and Anathoth in Israel. Beth-Anath, known today as Ain Aata has Roman temples and cult sites linked to Mount Hermon where the Bene-Elohim or sons of God came to earth, took a vow, and began marrying human women. This adds an interesing connection between Anath who was an alleged mother of a Nephilim with a site dedicated to the angelic parents of the Nephilim. Anath is also associated with a Book of Enoch watcher angel called Anathiel.

Haniel is first seen in Numbers 34:23 ESV which reads, *"Of the people of Joseph: of the tribe of the people of Manasseh a chief, Hanniel the son of Ephod."* Haniel is also seen in 1 Chronicles 7:39 ESV which states, *"The sons of Ulla: Arah, Hanniel, and Rizia."* While used as a man's name, the name Haniel is a female name that means "grace of God" or "joy of God."

Haniel is considered to be the angel that took Enoch up to God instead of dying in Genesis 5:24. It is considered by Rabbis that Haniel drives the chariot of fire that carried away Elijah to heaven as some of the accounts of how Enoch was taken by God were done (allegedly) in the same manner by a chariot of fire. There is mixing of views as to whether Haniel is male or female in the story, but many opinions point to female. Due to being spiritual beings, angels are not really either gender as gender is applied to purposes for reproduction. Angels use gender either when they fall and have sexual relationships with mankind, or when they see need to reveal themselves in a male or female form for ministry, prophecy, or other purposes.

Enoch made reference to the host of angels that he possibly saw before or after he went to heaven. This is found in his prophecy of Jude 1:14 ESV which says, *"It was also about these that Enoch, the seventh from Adam, prophesied, saying, "Behold, the Lord comes with ten thousand of his holy ones."* Holy ones is mixed in translation as some Bible translations identify holy ones as saints (humans) while others say angels.

The Orthodox Jewish Bible uses the Hebrew word *Malachim* in Jude 1:14 meaning angels or messengers. The book of Enoch mentions that Enoch witnessed seeing multitudes of angels such as the *Chayot, Ophanim, Seraphim, Cherubim,* and the *Galgallim.* This was after Enoch had been in the presence of the Shekinah or manifestation of God's glory, which is the Holy Spirit. The description of seeing the description of these angels by Enoch is similar to the description of the prophet Ezekiel's vision of the glory of the Lord and the throne of God mentioned in Ezekiel 1:4-28.

Venus is considered the morning and evening star in the Bible. The periods of Venus as evening and morning star each average about 263 days. In between, Venus disappears from view on the near side of the sun for about eight days, and it disappears from view on the far side of the sun for about fifty days, for a total of 584 days for the entire cycle.

Venus is the third brightest luminary in earth's sky. Only the sun and the moon are brighter. For certain long periods of time, Venus is bright enough to cast shadows on the Earth. Venus's cloud covering is highly reflective. It reflects about 70 percent of incoming sunlight back into space. That is part of the reason for Venus's brightness. The other primary reason is due to its closeness to Earth.

Venus has phases like the moon. It waxes and wanes. Hence, there are the phases of full Venus, half Venus, quarter Venus, crescent Venus, etc. What is the surprising part is that Venus appears to those on earth to be at its brightest when its phase is at a quarter or less.

Venus appears brighter as it gets closer to earth. When Venus is 'full' it is because it is on the opposite side of the sun. That makes it the farthest possible distance from the Earth. As the orbits of Earth and Venus bring them closer to the same side of the sun, Venus appears brighter-even when only a quarter Venus or less is seen.

There is an event called a Venus Transit. It is when Venus can be seen directly passing in front of the sun. This is similar to when the moon passes in front of the sun making a solar eclipse. Unlike the moon, which covers most of the sun, Venus appears as a small dot crossing the face of the sun. A transit or passage can only occur with the inner planets of Mercury and Venus because they are the only two planets that lie between Earth and the sun during their orbits. The year 2012 had a Venus transit. There is also a rare event called 'Venus Transits" which are pairs of transits that occur eight years apart from each other every 250 years.

The English word *Friday* is derived from the Anglo – Saxon word *Frigedaeg,* which means "Venus day." Many other languages trace their Friday from root words for or meaning "Venus day." In Spanish, the name for Friday is *Viernes.* The angel name Haniel is possibly derived from the Hebrew word *hana'ah* meaning delight, joy, enjoyment, or pleasure. The symbol or seal for Hana'ah is a crescent moon with a small dove beneath it. Combined with the word *el* for God is where "joy of God" then comes.

There is vast belief that angels are attributed to planets. Looking at history and modern times has shown a unique idea about angels and planets. Sigils painted or inscribed with angel names that are used in Jewish and occult practices often resemble something most never actually consider.[17] The art or symbols that represent angels resemble star constellations.

In the 1994 science fiction movie *Stargate*, Dr. Daniel Jackson (played by James Spader) is an Egyptologist hired by the United States Air Force to decipher an ancient Egyptian cover stone that had hieroglyphics on it that was not associated with ancient Egypt. After two weeks of getting nowhere, Dr. Jackson looked at a newspaper with a star constellation on it and connected the dots that the pictographs on the cover stone wasn't ancient writing, but instead were ancient symbols or sigils of star constellations. It is very likely that many symbols used with angel names

---

[17] Sigil- an inscribed or painted symbol considered having magical powers. Examples include seals and sigils of kings such as the Seal of Solomon or the ring of King Xerxes of Persia

shares the same idea of star constellations, or even planetary alignments due to angels being identified with certain planets.

Angels, planets, and symbols became associated with magic somewhere in history when people began to either listen to the wrong spirits, or were made by the ideas of a man or woman for their own purposes. Isaiah 8:19 ESV says, *"And when they say to you, "Inquire of the mediums and the necromancers who chirp and mutter," should not a people inquire of their God? Should they inquire of the dead on behalf of the living?"* People will find and use whatever they can to either attain power, look for answers, or both.

Many times people will seek the answers of the spirit through mediums and oracles. The ironic thing is that many of these so-called spirit microphones (mediums) can have spirits speaking through them. These are very likely evil spirits or even fallen angels. Galatians 3:19 ESV states, *"Why then the law? It was added because of transgressions, until the offspring should come to whom the promise had been made, and it was put in place through angels by an intermediary."*

Angels can use people to get things done. Both angels of light and dark use intermediaries to get their agendas across.

The parent angels of the Nephilim, the *Bene Elohim*, were said to have taught mankind about magic, star worship, and other mystic arts. The Nephilim themselves were said to be star worshipers. It was one reason they (according to biblical, historical, and archaeological accounts) kept their homes on or near mountains and caves for astronomy and astrology purposes. 2 Timothy 4:3-4 ESV reads, *"For the time is coming when people will not endure sound teaching, but having itching ears they will accumulate for themselves teachers to suit their own passions, And will turn away from listening to the truth and wander off into myths."* People have and always will be attracted to the things of the supernatural. The question to ask is what kind of damage will occur when a person becomes involved with the wrong beings of the supernatural?

CHAPTER 13: LAST REVELATION

Angels can be seen as male and female. Their representation is dependent on the situation, their nature, or how they wish to present themselves. They have appeared all throughout the Bible, history, and stories the world over. The most important thing to understand is whether or not they represent God, fallen, Lucifer, or the human sinful spirit.

Not all fallen angels or spirits are loyal to Lucifer. Many of them are rebels loyal only to themselves. The depiction of certain angels is to show both literal and metaphorical imagery for specific reasons. Male and female angels and spirits can be viewed as both righteous and wicked. Some examples of women in the supernatural are representations of both past and present.

One example is seen in Revelation 12:1-6 ESV:

"And a great sign appeared in heaven: a woman clothed with the sun, with the moon under her feet, and on her head a crown of twelve stars. She was pregnant and was crying out in birth pains and the agony of giving birth. And another sign appeared in the heaven: behold a great red dragon, with seven heads and ten horns, and on his heads seven diadems. His tail swept down a third of the stars of heaven and cast them to the earth. And the dragon stood before the woman who was about to give birth, so that when she bore her child he might devour it. She gave birth to a male child, one who is to rule all the nations with a rod of iron, but her child was caught up to God and to His throne, and the woman fled into the wilderness, where she has a place prepared by God, in which she is to be nourished for 1,260 days."

The story is that of Satan and his rebellion against God, the future of Jesus as Shepherd with mankind as His sheep, and the bride (church) of God being protected from harm. Another interesting story found in Revelation is made in

*William Blake Painting of The Great Red Dragon and Woman Clothed With The Sun. Courtesy of Hohum

regards to the mother and wife of Nimrod, Semiramis.

Revelation 17:5 ESV says, *"And on her forehead was written a name of mystery: "Babylon the great, mother of prostitutes and of earth's abominations."* This scripture is often thought to represent the image or spirit of Semiramis who, as previously mentioned, is a famous Babylonian queen and figure among the Middle East.

The imagery of Semiramis in Revelation is similar to the imagery of Lilith in Isaiah 34. Revelation 18:1-2 ESV declares:

"After this I saw another angel coming down from heaven, having great authority, and the earth was made bright with his glory. And he called out with a mighty voice, Fallen, fallen is Babylon the great! She has become a dwelling place for demons, a haunt for every unclean spirit, a haunt for every unclean bird, a haunt for every unclean and detestable beast."

The representation of Babylon and the woman named Babylon the Great (Semiramis or her prostitute spirit) is the representation of the spirit prince (or princess) of Babylon. Isaiah 13:19 ESV reads, *"And Babylon, the glory of kingdoms, the splendor and pomp of the Chaldeans, will be like Sodom and Gomorrah when God overthrew them."* Like the Jezebel spirit, the Babylon spirit is one that brings about death and destruction from obsession, addiction, and prostitution.

It is possible that the representation of Babylon in league with female imagery is to show the principality that once presided over Babylon similar to the principalities of Persia and Greece found in the book of Daniel. Those types of spirits are more than just images or representations of entities. They are spiritual mentalities. A mentality is hard to break, as it requires both a head (mind) and heart change. Like breaking addictions, the only way to change a mentality is to break it completely.

Romans 12:1-2 ESV states:

"I appeal to you therefore, brothers, by the mercies of God, to present your bodies as a living sacrifice, holy and acceptable to God, which is your spiritual worship. Do not be conformed to this world, but be transformed by the renewal of your mind, that by testing you may discern what is the will of God, what is good and acceptable and perfect."

Whether dealing with male or female spirits, feminine or masculine mentalities, positive or negative influences, empowerment or entitlement, it is necessary to always recognize every spirit and be ready to combat them, break them, and remove them. That is the way of God and that is the way of His glory.

1 John 4:1 ESV says, *"Beloved, do not believe every spirit, but test the spirits to see whether they are from God, for many false prophets have gone out into the world."*

People need to be careful of what is out in the world. With so many news medias, social medias, radical rights movements, and religious trends coming to the forefront, and so many new doors opening up to spirits to come in and take root wherever they pop up, we must protect ourselves! God has given mankind the authority to think and act in the ways to conquer such manifestations. Luke 10:19 ESV states, *"Behold, I have given you authority to tread on serpents and scorpions, and over the power of the enemy, and nothing shall hurt you."* Humanity has the authority of God through the name of Jesus and the power of the Holy Spirit. They just have to be willing to walk in it fully.

It is important to remember that mankind doesn't just wage war against the devil, though he is the greatest adversary of God. He was the original architect of rebellion and the first angel ever to become fallen. Fallen is defined as one who is subject to sin or depravity.

Revelation 12:9 ESV says, *"And the great dragon was thrown down, that ancient serpent, who is called the devil and Satan, the deceiver of the whole world-he was thrown down to the earth, and his angels were thrown down with him."*

Lucifer was the first to rebel, but not alone, and not the last. His sins are a lesson to learn from as stated in 1 John 3:8

ESV:

"Whoever makes a practice of sinning is of the devil, for the devil has been sinning from the beginning. The reason the Son of God appeared was to destroy the works of the devil."

It is important to learn to see everything that comes before one's eyes. It is imperative to walk with a mind that knows how to see when it is tested so that one can pass the test. It is vital to guard one's heart so it can stay pure and positive. Galatians 6:7 ESV reads, *"Do not be deceived: God is not mocked, for whatever one sows, that will he also reap."*

When a person acts like God, then they are living as the image of God. If God is not mocked, then His image should choose not to be mocked too. Test the spirits, to know how to learn the differences of the things in the world. Trust God and the Holy Spirit to reveal all the things that will make a man more than a conqueror. If a someone is not willing to stand for God, they will fall for anything.

GLOSSARY

ABYSS- a deep or seemingly bottomless chasm. Some translations of regions of hell are conceived as a bottomless pit such as "Satan's dark abyss."

AEOTOS- Greek word for eagle. The "Aeotos Dios" is translated from Greek into "Eagle of Zeus." The eagle is considered one of the first creations by the Greek goddess Gaia.

DUALISM- the division of something conceptually into two opposed or contrasted aspects, or the state of being divided.

FEMINISM- the Advocacy of women's rights on the basis of the equality of the sexes.

HUMANISM- an outlook or system of thought attaching prime importance to human rather than divine or supernatural matters. Humanist beliefs stress the potential value and goodness of human beings, emphasize common human needs, and seek solely rational ways of solving human problems.

ISIS- Egyptian goddess of nature and magic.

MAAT- Egyptian goddess of truth, justice, and cosmic order, daughter of the sun god Ra. Word or name of Maat literally means 'truth.'

MONISM- a theory or doctrine that denies the existence of a distinction or duality in some sphere, such as that between matter and mind, or God and the world.

NECROMANCY- the supposed practice of communicating with the dead, especially in order to predict the future.

NESHER- Hebrew name meaning eagle or vulture.

NEW AGE- a broad movement characterized by alternative approaches to traditional Western culture, with an interest in spirituality, mysticism, holism, and environmentalism.

ORACLE- a priest or priestess acting as a medium through whom advice or prophecy was sought from the gods in classical antiquity. A response or message given by an oracle, typically one that is ambiguous or obscure.

OREB- Hebrew name meaning raven or crow.

PSALTER- the Book of Psalms. A copy of the biblical Psalms, especially for liturgical use.

PROGENITOR- a person or thing from which a person, animal, or plant is descended or originates; an ancestor or parent.

PSYCHOPATH- a person suffering from chronic mental disorder with abnormal or violent social behavior.

SOCIOPATH- a person with a personality disorder manifesting itself in extreme antisocial attitudes and behavior and a lack of conscience.

SORCERY- the use of power gained from the assistance or control of evil spirits for divining. The use of magic, especially black magic.

SPIRITUALISM- a system of belief or religious practice based on supposed communication with the spirits of the dead, especially through mediums.

WITCHCRAFT- the practice of magic, especially black magic; the use of spells and the invocation of spirits.

WICCA- a form of modern paganism, especially a tradition founded in England in the mid 20th century and claiming its origins in pre-Christian religions.

BIBLIOGRAPHY

Abegg Jr., Martin, and Cook, Edward, Wise, Michael, *The Dead Sea Scrolls.* New York, NY: Harper Collins Publishing, 2005.

Adler, Margot, *Drawing Down the Moon: Witches, Druids, Goddess-Worshippers, and Other Pagans in America Today, Revised and Expanded Edition.* Beacon Press. 1986

Ancient Nephilim ooparts-Marib Dam Worked for 1,000 Years. 2014. www.fallenangels-ckquarterman.com/ancient-nephilim-ooparts-marib-dam-worked-1000-years/.

Archangel Anael-Angelic & Planetary Correspndences. 2018. www.archangels-and-angels.com/aa_pages/correspondences_planet/archangel_anael.html.

ARIEL. 2018. HTTPS://WWW.BIBLESTUDYTOOLS.COM/DICTIONARY/ARIEL/.

Asherah: The Tree of Life. 2015. Tokinwoman.blogspot.com/2015/06/asherah-tree-of-life.html?m+1.

Bacher, Wilhelm; Prince, John Dyneley; M. Seligsohn. "Teraphim."*JewishEncyclopedia.*1906.www.jewishencyclopedia.com/articles/14331-teraphim.

Bahn, Paul, Ed. *The Complete Illustrated History of World Archaeology.* Blaby Road, Wingston Leicestershire: Lorenz Books, 2013.

Bertrand, Azra, *Dream Temples, Mary Magdalene & Pirestesses of Astarte.* 2016. https://www.thefountainoflife.org/12387-2/.

Bøgh, Birgitte, *Beyond Nock: From Adhesion to Conversion in the Mystery Cults.* History of Religions. 2015

Burton, Judd H., *Chemosh: the Ancient God of the Moabites*. 2018. https://www.thoughtco.com/chemosh-lord-of-the-moabites-117630.

Donnelly, Deirdre E., Morrison, Patrick J., Hereditary Gigantism-the biblical giant Goliath and his brothers. 2014. https://www.ncbi.nlm.nih.gov/pmc/articles/PMC4113151/.

Egypt Unveils 4,400-year-old-tomb of ancient priestess. 2018. www.bbc.com/news/world-middle-east-42931533.

Flaherty, Thomas H. ed., *"The Pioneers of Civilization." Sumer: Cities of Eden.* 158-159. Richmond, Virginia: Time Life Books, 1993.

Gordon, Cyrus H., *The Ancient Near East.* New York, NY: Ventor Publishers, Inc., 1965.

Grudem, Wayne, *The English Standard Version Study Bible.* Wheaton, IL: Crossway, 2008.

Hekate. 2018. www.darkmother.com/hekate.html.

Hopler, Whitney. *Chayot Ha Kodesh Angels.* 2018. https://www.thoughtco.com/chayot-ha-kodesh-angels-123902.

Jastrow Jr., Morris, Howell, Toy, Crawford Howell, Jastrow, Marcus, Ginzberg, Louis, Hokler, Kaufman, *Ashes.* 2011. www.jewishencyclopedia.com/articles/1944-ashes.

Mazar, Amihai, *Archaeology of The Land of The Bible- 10,000-586 B.C.E.* New York, NY: Doubleday, 1992.

Mondesir, Desiree M. *Exploring Jezebel's Family Tree: Baal & The Queen of Heaven Part I.* 2018. www.desireemmondesir.com/home/2015/2/27/exploring-jezebelz-family-tree-baal-the-queen-of-heaven-part-I.

Mondesir, Desiree M. *Exploring Jezebel's Family Tree: Baal & The Queen of Heaven Part II*. 2018. www.desireemmondesir.com/home/2015/2/27/exploring-jezebelz-family-tree-baal-the-queen-of-heaven-part-II.

Mondesir, Desiree M. *Exploring Jezebel's Family Tree: Baal & The Queen of Heaven Part III*. 2018. www.desireemmondesir.com/home/2015/2/27/exploring-jezebelz-family-tree-baal-the-queen-of-heaven-part-III.

Myth/Hebrew Mythology. 2018. Tvtropes.org/pmwiki/pmwiki.php/Myth/HebrewMytholog.

New International Version, *Life Application Study Bible*. Grand Rapids, MI: Zondervan. 2011.

Occurrence of the Stars. 2018. https://mongolianstore.com/astronomical-knowledge-2/.

Of Myth and the Bible: Part 10 The Lion Men of Moab. 2015. https://godawa.com/myth-bible-part-10-lion-men-moab/.

Oral Roberts Edition. *Holy Bible King James Version*. Tulsa, OK: Oral Roberts Evangelistic Association, Inc., 1981.

Phoenix (mythology). 2015. www.newworldencyclopedia.org/entry/Phoenix_(mythology).

PHOENIX: Seeing if Job 29:18/Bible Shows Fiery Mythological Bird as fact or Fiction. 2012. https://www.christianforums.com/threads/phoenix-seeing-if-job-29-18-bible-shows-fiery-mythological-bird-as-fact-or-fiction.7640113/.

Propolos, Hekate. *Ancient Necromantic Practices in Averno*. 2016. Awitchalone.com/crossroads/index.php?post/201609/27/Ancient-Necromantic-Practices-in-Averno.

Reisch, Robyn, *6 Physical Effects of Heartbreak.* 2018.
Iheartintelligence.com/2017/03/20/6-physical-effects-of-heartbreak/.

Seals of Solomon. 1898.
https://www.themysticdreamacademy.com/seals-of-solomon/.

Stern, David H., *The Complete Jewish Bible.* Baltimore, Maryland:
Lederer Messianic Publications, 1998.

The English Standard Version Study Bible. Wheaton, IL: Crossway,
2008.

The Jewish Milcham Bird is the Legend of the Phoenix. 2015.
https://onthehillgilayjun.blogspot.com/2015/06/the-jewish-milcham-bird-is-legend-of.html?m=1.

The Orthodox Jewish Bible Fourth Edition. New York, NY: AFI
International Publishers, 2011.

What We Belive About Addictions. 2018.
https://rurecovery.com/believe-addictions/.

Witchcraft and Sorcery. 2012.
Bet-ilim.blogspot.com/2012/01/witchcraft-and-sorcery.html?m+1

PHOTO SOURCES

Pg. 88 photos courtesy of Smerdis of Ton PD-US, Taron Sabaryan PD-US

Pg. 89 photos courtesy of Dbachmann PD-US, Liftarn PD-US

Pg. 90 photos courtesy of Jsbaw7160 PD-US, Sarukinu PD-US

Pg. 91 photos courtesy of Byam Shaw PD-US, D. Martynov PD-US

Pg. 92 photos courtesy of Vincent Stenberg CC0-1.0, Camocon PD-US

Pg. 100 photo courtesy of Ckroberts61 CC-BY-2.0

Pg. 120 photo courtesy of Eloquence PD-US

Pg. 124 photo courtesy of Adam JonesPHD CC-BY-SA 2.0

Pg. 130 photo courtesy of Eli+ PD-US

Pg. 135 photo courtesy of Gryffindor CC0-0.1

Pg. 143 photo courtesy of Alan D. Wilson CC-BY-SA-2.5

Pg. 164 photo courtesy of Humus Sapiens PD-US

Pg. 171 photos courtesy of Calimeronte CC-BY-3.0

Pg. 177 photos courtesy of Securinger CC-BY-SA-3.0, Jpb 1301 CC-BY-SA-3.0

Pg. 192 photo courtesy of Hobum PD-US

ABOUT THE AUTHOR

Dr. Harry Assad Salem III is an author of several books dealing with theology, archaeology, religion, history, and science. He holds state, regional, national, and world championships in the sports of powerlifting and strongman. He is also an NPC bodybuilder.

Dr. Salem holds five doctorate degrees in the fields of theology, archaeology, Biblical studies, Christian education, and practical ministry. He has been involved in ministry since the age of thirteen with Salem Family Ministries. He has lectured at School of Worship for several years. He has developed a children's book series called Prayer Buddies with two books published called Count of Ten Say Amen and Ten Steps to Build and be Spirit Filled.

Dr. Salem is an advocate of education who believes that the highest goals one can achieve can be reached through knowledge and skills learned in the classroom or on the job, and applied in the world to gain experience and mastery over anything and everything. Dr. Salem's personal motto and creed is, "Excellence is excellent." It is a belief that has kept him thriving for the highest of excellence in every pursuit he has worked towards. He hopes to inspire others to achieve their own pursuits of excellence, foster climates of change in their lives, and live to their fullest potential in everyway possible. He has one niece, Mia Gabrielle Salem, and one nephew, Roman Harry Salem Jr.

I would love to hear from you. There are many ways to stay connected to me. You can contact me either through the mail or the internet at the ministry website.

Salem Family Ministries

P.O. Box 1595

Cathedral City, CA 92234

www.salemfamilyministries.org

www.ingramcontent.com/pod-product-compliance
Lightning Source LLC
Chambersburg PA
CBHW071216090426
42736CB00014B/2851